A gift from
Project ♥ HEART
A Partnerships in Character Education Grant
An investment in you for your work with students

Just When I Needed You

*True Stories of Adults
Who Made a Difference
in the Lives of Young People*

Written and edited by

DEBORAH FISHER

Search
INSTITUTE

*Practical research
benefiting children
and youth*

Dedicated to Gerry Colon, the first teacher to tap this writer's heart

**Just When I Needed You: True Stories of
Adults Who Made a Difference in the Lives of Young People**

Deborah Fisher

Copyright © 2004 Search Institute

Search Institute^{SM} and Developmental Assets^{TM} are trademarks of Search Institute.

10 9 8 7 6 5 4 3 2 1
Printed on acid-free paper in the United States of America

Search Institute
615 First Avenue Northeast, Suite 125 • Minneapolis, MN 55413
www.search-institute.org
612-376-8955 • 800-888-7828

ISBN: 1-57482-843-6

Credits
Editor: Kathryn L. Hong
Production Coordinator: Mary Ellen Buscher
Book Design and Composition: Wendy Holdman, Stanton Publication Services, Inc.
Cover Design: Percolator
Cover Illustration: Marie Olofsdotter

Library of Congress Cataloging-in-Publication Data

Fisher, Deborah, 1951–
    Just when I needed you : true stories of adults who made a difference in the lives of young people / written and edited by Deborah Fisher.
        p.   cm.
    ISBN 1-57482-843-6 (pbk. : alk. paper)
    1. Teenagers and adults—Case studies. 2. Interpersonal relations in adolescence—Case studies. 3. Teenagers—United States—Biography. I. Title.
HQ799.2.A35F57   2004
305.235—dc22   2004012620

Contents

Unhistoric Acts

Stories of adults who helped young people
to connect, fit in, and overcome obstacles

An Old-Fashioned Apprenticeship

Stories of adults who taught young people
about life and wisdom through their own work

Simple Gifts

Stories of adults who reached out in a
small way and made a huge difference

Close to Home

Stories of exceptional parents, grandparents, and aunts and uncles in ordinary and extraordinary circumstances

Giving Back

Stories from adults who make giving to young people a core part of their life—and gain much in return

Acknowledgments

⤚

Born with the uncontrollable impulse to write, I've been lucky enough to make a career out of telling stories. The folks at Search Institute in particular have been kind enough to give me lots of wonderful opportunities to indulge myself. So I must continue to thank, first and foremost, Peter Benson and all the dedicated people at Search for developing and sustaining this work of positively supporting young people. Writing about what has become my favorite subject continues to bring deep joy into my life.

As a result of the varied projects I've worked on for Search over the last six years, I have come in contact with many tireless, enthusiastic asset builders from all over the country. I thank that ever-widening circle of friends who sustain me daily as we all work to build a better life for the young people around us. These folks and many more out there with whom I chat via the phone or Internet always share generously whenever I ask for help and teach me much in their sharing. I am pleased to include some of their stories in this book.

I want to thank my editor, Kay Hong, for trusting me with this project and giving me the chance to delve into such riches. Kay embodies just the right combination of pushing, pulling, cheerleading, and letting go that helps a writer get the job done. Her steely-eyed professional gaze has also helped me grow tremendously as a writer at a time when I was ready to stretch.

I would also like to acknowledge the people who are named in these stories. Some of them have already left this world, but the impact they made is revealed in these stories. I like to imagine that there will be a few scenes, played out among those who are still present, of being handed this book by the person who told their story. A heartfelt thank-you for the contribution you have made, and continue to make, in the lives of young people.

To everyone who contributed a story for this book a very humble thank-you. I did not so much write these stories as work collaboratively with each person to bring his or her thoughts, experiences, and lessons to fruition. I was touched by each story and enjoyed getting to know each contributor on a deeper level.

I want to thank also my generous, tolerant friends—old and new—who allowed me to pick through their pasts, poking and prodding them with questions so I could write about their stories for this project.

Introduction

During the writing of this book, dozens of people spoke to me of moments in their lives when someone made a real difference:

- The teenage boy hiding in the dark of his home to escape the Nazis, having long conversations with his mother about justice and compassion.

- The young woman introduced to the spirit of a river by a knowledgeable, insightful adult friend.

- The little girl meeting for the first time the woman who would become her lifelong mentor, friend, and traveling companion to Paris.

- A boy at a crossroads in his life whose coach laid a hand on his shoulder and asked him a critical question.

Some of the turning points described in this book were the result of deliberate actions taken by a thoughtful adult, but just as many were simple, spontaneous gestures. What happened in each and every one of these stories is that, for a significant moment, a young person received an adult's undivided attention, and a change took place. These are the stories of cherished people who stood out in both troubled and untroubled lives, people who reached out to touch—even save—a young person.

Many adults express concern about young people in today's culture and feel that preparing them for the future should be our number-one priority, but many also admit they don't really know what sort of role they can or should play to have a positive impact on young people's lives. Even when adults do have some ideas about what to do, they don't always feel they have permission to do it. Personal reticence and perceived cultural barriers often prevent adults from reaching out to young people. Yet it's vital that we do so.

In *Others People's Kids*, Peter Scales describes why it's important for all adults, not just parents and professionals, to be involved in the lives of children and adolescents. Research shows us that young people develop better when they have a variety of positive relationships with adults outside their own families. They have the potential to exceed mere competence and to thrive, becoming more emotionally healthy, socially competent, academically successful, and optimistic about their future.

This research is based, in part, on the work conducted by Search Institute over the last two decades on what are called *Developmental Assets*. Think of these Developmental Assets (see pages 155–57) as the "nutrients" of healthy development for children and teens. The more of the assets young people have, the less likely they are to engage in risky behaviors and the more positive choices they will make. The great majority of these important nutrients—positive experiences, skills, opportunities, qualities, and values—are best provided to young people through relationships with caring, responsible adults. In fact, the more healthy, positive relationships a child has with adults, the better.

So how do we help ourselves and each other to set aside any doubts and take the risks that we know in our hearts will help young people grow? How do we encourage other adults to take those actions that Scales calls the gathering of the molecules into a web of connection that can lead to change? We tell them stories.

"Such stories," writes Scales, "remind people that change is possible and that they can make a difference, even if only for one person."

Since we humans first started huddling around campfires, we have used stories to bind us together, to teach, to entertain, to share, to pass down, to connect. "Stories are medicine," writes Clarissa Pinkola Estes in *Women Who Run with the Wolves*. "They have such power."

The powerful stories in this book are gathered to inspire and instruct all of us in the myriad ways we adults can be present in the lives of children and youth. Some of the stories are about actions that were very dramatic; some involve moments that were extremely simple and small. I wrote many of the stories from interviews and notes, but some people communicated such a strong voice when they sent me their own written drafts of their remembrances that I merely edited and introduced their stories, keeping them in first person to preserve their freshness and immediacy. From the tale of a teacher who saw past a young person's doubts to her talent, to that of the aunt and uncle sitting down to listen to a nephew pondering his possible futures, each of these stories reveals the heart of a person who made a difference along the way. The people in these stories learned something, and now we can learn from them.

Fueling the Fire Within

There is an often-shared quotation from Goethe that talks about the transformation that takes place when you treat someone not just as they are, but as they ought to be—they become what they *could* be. Some adults just seem to have a knack for seeing deeply into a young person and helping to bring out what could be. Like experts examining a diamond in the rough, these teachers and guides detect a talent, a skill, a passion that the child may not yet be aware of. The storytellers in this section recount how several extraordinary adults saw the as-yet-unrealized facets within them as young people and found creative ways to help them see it in themselves.

Preacher

~

Dumas, Arkansas, was the last chance for Kareem Moody. His parents were divorced and, after moving from Houston to Killeen, Texas, and spending summers with his dad in Chicago, the growing 14-year-old was starting to get into trouble. Kareem's mom decided to pack him up with his two sisters and move them to the small southern town of Dumas, population about 10,000, to help care for her dying grandfather and to get Kareem into a different environment.

Even before he started hanging around basketball courts (and never getting picked for the team), Kareem dreamed of going to college and playing ball. Recalling Dumas High School's basketball team, Kareem laughs. "If you were 6'2" in 1988, you were automatically a center." He wasn't very good at the sport, but he got involved and started getting playing time. He also started to be friends with the other players, and they pushed each other to compete not only in basketball, but also in the classroom. "There was already a lot of tradition in this high school community when I arrived, and I seemed to fit into the puzzle," Kareem remembers.

It wasn't until his 10th-grade year that Kareem started to notice the man sitting in the stands for every game, watching him. It wasn't just that he was an older white man in a sea of black faces—it was the way he watched Kareem play. He was always emotional, alternately cheering or grimacing depending on how play went. No one on the team knew anything about him. He never showed up in the usual places that other team fans did, such as the locker room. He always just sat in the same spot, in the black section of the gym, and focused on Kareem's game. He had some reason for being there. The players took to calling him Preacher.

Preacher was always there—at every home game, at state tournaments, even traveling as far as 200 miles to watch the team play on competitors' courts. "I could feel his eyes on me, and the way it felt to me, my games didn't just all run together. It mattered to somebody what I did *that* day." Kareem didn't look for the old man, but he'd notice if he wasn't there. "We'd have conversations about him," says Kareem. "Nothing really formal, but wondering who he was. Who is that old man? Is the old man there? Somebody would say, 'He's Moody's fan.'"

Near the end of his 10th-grade year, Kareem found himself in Preacher's vicinity at the end of a game. As they passed each other, the old man said, "You know, you could play college ball." Preacher had touched upon Kareem's deepest unspoken desire. "It was almost mystical. I was still struggling at that point, but I felt he was critiquing me, almost like he was a scout. He kind of tricked me in a way. I started to think that maybe I *could* play at the next level."

Kareem started playing more and more, and while he made more mistakes, he also got better and better. By his senior year, Kareem was a star of the team, receiving lots of local press and recognition for his play. He finally knew he was good enough to be recruited to play college ball, and after getting several offers, he accepted a scholarship at Henderson State University in Arkansas.

College ball was fun but exhausting enough to make Kareem realize that he didn't want to try and crack the NBA. While college had originally been about playing basketball, during his sophomore year, Kareem began to focus more on academics and felt increasingly confident about pursuing a degree. "I started to feel like I belonged, and I rode it out."

Graduating with a degree in communications, Kareem began working as a gang coordinator in Little Rock, Arkansas, using his gift of gab to coax gang members off the street and back into school. Kareem is now the program director at Positive Atmosphere Reaches Kids (P.A.R.K.), a comprehensive after-school program in Little Rock for at-risk youth in grades 8 through 12. His experience with his one elderly fan still inspires him.

"Even now, Preacher kind of fuels the fire in me," says Kareem. "With that one comment, he got me to step up and work hard. Now I try to be creative with some of the young people I work with and give them the same sort of pat on the back that that old man gave me."

Kareem describes his work at P.A.R.K. as "stopping 'em at the gate and turning 'em around." "First I try to connect with each young person. I've got one young man who likes to dance, and even though I'm more into sports myself, I try to pump up what *he* wants to do. I try to find something about every one of the kids that come through here and start with that connection. I let them know it matters to me that they're there that day, then I pat them on the back and try to 'trick' them, the way Preacher tricked me, into doing whatever they think they want to do. That's what he did for me."

Kareem Moody is still a basketball player. He has started a business promoting street basketball and self-publishes one newsletter that highlights local talent and another for parents. He loves telling stories and motivating people, especially hard-to-reach youth.

Pamela Widman explains how
one teacher's unwavering support
changed her perspective.

PAMELA WIDMAN

An Accidental Compliment

"You're very perceptive," my teacher, Carol Gianfrancisco, commented during a private detention—which, by the way, I didn't deserve.

"Yeah, well, so are you!" I continued to stare out the window while I spoke my retort with as much hatred as I could muster. I was 12 years old, and it was 1974, my first year at the Holy Ghost School in Illinois after attending public school for several years. If she was allowed to call me names, I could use the same word against her, even if I didn't know what it meant.

"Thank you." She smiled and went back to her work. Her smile seemed so fake.

Of course, I went home and looked up the word—and it meant something nice! She was complimenting me, and I had complimented her back! I hadn't meant to be nice to her. That night, I pledged to be severely disruptive in class the next day to make up for the accidental compliment.

However, no matter what I did the next day, that teacher ignored me until she found some stupid little thing to praise me for. It was dumb, and it only made me hate her more. She was trying to manipulate me, I could tell. "No teacher ever really likes me," I thought to myself. "They just want me to be quiet and do their stupid worksheets."

Yes, I had an attitude problem. Sixth grade was a tough year. There was nothing really wrong at home, but I craved more attention. My brother had been my best friend for as long as I could remember, and we used to play sports together—until he discovered girls, and then I wasn't much fun for him anymore.

I didn't have much self-esteem. I was extremely creative, but I felt "odd." I had a smart mouth. I read books while my siblings watched *Creature Features*. During my previous school year, another teacher stood me in front of the class to put me down. "She thinks she's so smart, but really she will be the biggest loser when she's all grown up" were his exact words. I tried to tell myself that *he* was the loser, but another part of me was afraid that he was right. I was already smoking, swearing, and kissing boys under the library tables.

This new teacher was different. I just couldn't rile her, but she could rile me, all right. Sometimes she made me do my work three times until it was just so. She could tell I was coasting through the work, but she couldn't prove it, and I hated her for making me do it again.

By the end of the first year, I decided my life would be over if I ever had to have her again. Actually, I ended up having her for math, science, and religion over the next three years. Her expectations were high, her patience was unlimited, her smiles were constant, and I just couldn't fight it that long. Getting her attention for positive behavior became almost addictive. I wanted to shine, to be someone, and finally to participate and make a difference at the school and in my church.

By the middle of my second year with her, I was teaching her to play the guitar, and she was teaching me to love Shakespeare and the digestive system. Her prodding pushed me into the highest classes in all subjects by my freshman year in high school, and I eventually evolved into a true community leader.

I didn't start out to be a teacher when I began my career path, but when my youngest son started school, I took a part-time job as a program assistant for gifted education in the school district so I could have some days off. Eventually I found myself writing grants and guest teaching in creative dramatics, geography, and writing. I started to feel that maybe I could make a bigger difference to children and give back to some of the troubled ones if I went into the classroom full-time.

I'm now in my second year of teaching 6th grade (of course!) at Liberty Middle School in Aurora, Colorado. Last year, Carol was a guest teacher in my classroom. She still has that "magic," and I *still* feel special every time I'm with her.

I teach more than 150 students a day, and I can tell when one walks into my classroom with a headache or a heartache. From Carol, I learned to look for the slightest positive things to praise in children who are struggling, to figure out what lights them up, and to help them build on that. I try to have high expectations without pity. Every day, I want my students to know that I care about them and love being with them.

— Pamela Widman lives in Centennial, Colorado, with her husband of 20 years and two sons, 13 and 16 years old. She is currently in graduate school for writing. Once a professional actress, Pamela now plays characters in her classroom to keep students interested in things like punctuation. In the summer she rolls down the windows of her car and screams along with her music CDs—even at stoplights. She dreams of owning a Harley.

Music Lessons

～

Nancy Stevens grew up in Roanoke, Virginia, as the youngest of three children with two very annoyingly talented older brothers, Scott and Neil Brown. In 1979, 8-year-old Nancy was reluctant to take piano lessons, but because her brothers were doing well at it, she was required to take piano lessons, too.

Piano lessons were taught by Nan, a friend of Nancy's mom and, in fact, Nancy's godmother. Nan was a very tall, stern German woman who had escaped from the Nazis. Her house was very neat and tidy and full of photos of her four children, who would all grow up to be doctors and lawyers. "She was very nice," recalls Nancy, "but also demanding as a teacher. She was driven to make sure that others around her were successful in whatever they did. She scared me a little bit."

Nancy liked playing the piano, and the lessons were fun when Nan was pleased, but the little girl was impatient. She wanted to play "Moonlight Sonata" while her teacher was still trying to help her learn the basics of "Mary Had a Little Lamb." So Nancy found it difficult to make herself practice the simple songs.

One fall day Nancy arrived ill prepared to demonstrate her lesson, but she didn't want to admit that she had not practiced, so she struck upon what seemed like a brilliant idea: she would lie. "I was a kid with a creative mind," remembers Nancy. "I wasn't really a liar, but I thought by telling a little one, it would keep me out of trouble." When Nan asked her if she had practiced, she would just say she had hurt her thumb, and that would be that.

But when Nancy tried out her plan, she faced an unexpected response. "This will be challenging for you, then," said Nan, "because now you'll have to learn to play this piece without your thumb." "That hour was living hell," says Nancy, laughing. "Playing the piano without your thumb is like driving a stick-shift vehicle with only one hand. I spent the whole hour confused and frustrated. I could also feel that Nan relished the fact that she'd caught me in a lie. I had to work much harder than I would have originally."

Despite the arduous hour, Nancy still had not quite learned her lesson. The next week she decided to try to preserve her 8-year-old dignity by keeping the story going a little longer, maintaining that her thumb was better but still sore. Nancy suffered through yet another hour of thumbless practice.

"It was a very tricky and very smart thing she did," says Nancy, "because I finally learned that making excuses to get out of something means doing a lot more work in the long run."

Nancy now works as a psychologist and often uses the small lesson she learned about truth to help her provide more effective support for her clients in her practice. "I realize now that sometimes people will try to tell you a little lie to cover up the larger, more important issues. The little lies are like warning signals. I've learned to look past the little lies that people tell and help them focus on the heart of the bigger issues."

Nancy Stevens lives in the Blue Ridge Mountains with her husband, Phill, an artist/musician, and their boxer, Ty. She went on to take more piano lessons and eventually took flute lessons with a very demanding teacher from Julliard, who, after the experience with Nan, did not intimidate Nancy at all.

GABRIELE BENDISTIS AND
MARTHA GRIECO

Let Me Introduce Myself

It's Martha Grieco's job as Community Outreach Liaison for Riddle Memorial Hospital in Media, Pennsylvania, to help teens connect with new people and experiences, but it's also her passion. "I don't see reaching out to young people as taking a 'risk,' but just natural behavior and very humbling," says Martha. "I always learn from youth, and I truly enjoy spending time and sharing ideas with them." Martha's "natural behavior" includes careful observation of the young people she meets as part of her work facilitating the region's Healthy Communities Initiative (HCI), a network of organizations and individuals supporting young people in Media, Upper Providence, Middletown, and Edgmont, Pennsylvania.

At a community fundraiser several years ago, Martha Grieco recognized a young woman going around the room selling raffle tickets as a student from Penncrest High School. Always looking for youth to get involved with HCI, Martha introduced herself to 16-year-old Gabriele Bendistis and, learning of her interest in sports, invited her to an upcoming meeting about how to develop and publicize sports clinics for younger children in the community.

Gabriele didn't know what to expect, but she accepted the invitation. "There weren't too many other kids at the first meeting," she recalls, "and it was kind of intimidating at first. The adults were all jumping right into the discussion, and I had no idea what the focus was. I was there to volunteer to run sports clinics for children, but everyone seemed to be talking about public relations. I didn't know what they were trying to promote, and I was afraid to ask. When Martha asked me later why I was so quiet, I said I didn't know what was going on. She cleared everything up and made it sound like it would be a lot of fun."

While it would be some time before the sports clinics actually got off the ground, it turned out that there was plenty to do to help publicize HCI. The meeting Gabriele attended was one of a series aimed at coming up with ideas for getting the word out about the initiative's efforts. Once Martha answered Gabriele's questions, Gabriele felt much more comfortable attending additional public relations meetings, especially when other young people started coming, too. "Martha would always ask me questions to get me to talk," says Gabriele. "Once I did talk, all the adults in the group were encouraging. Everyone's ideas were written on the board and no one ever said, 'That won't work.' I'd never had an experience working with adults like that before."

Martha was drawn to Gabriele from the beginning. "I've learned that many times the young people who initially seem shy or tentative are the ones with something significant to share. When we talked, she had some really great ideas for connecting with the media about our initiative's efforts, and it seemed as if she was trying to find her place in the group without being pushy. I asked her if she liked to write."

Martha had hit upon the perfect job for Gabriele—writing

about an upcoming inter-government seminar at which political and community leaders from four townships were invited to learn about HCI. The seminar was designed and delivered by local youth. Gabriele was the initiative's "reporter," assigned to interview community leaders and write several articles for local newspapers. Gabriele had always liked writing in school, but she had never done anything like this.

Martha suggested to Gabriele that she introduce herself to people in the room during the event, asking them if she could interview them for her story after the seminar. "I started by introducing her to some people to get her comfortable with the protocol and then watched as she smoothly moved around the 75 invited guests doing exactly what she had to do."

Gabriele found that she actually knew many people from her work at a local restaurant. Between her own contacts and Martha's introductions, everyone she talked to responded to her very positively, giving her good feedback. The articles she wrote for the local *County Press* and *Town Talk* were so successful that Martha sent a copy of Gabriele's story to the county's largest newspaper, the *Daily Times,* which printed the young journalist's piece with her first byline. "That was really cool," says Gabriele.

Gabriele discovered that she had a new passion. "I never expected my first time writing an article to be so well received. Now I'm the 'reporter' for HCI. But I also got a lot more confidence in my friendship with Martha. She started by introducing me to people, and now I can do that for myself. Trying something new definitely changed what I thought of my abilities."

Gabriele's newfound role with HCI has not only boosted her self-confidence, but has made her more visible in her community and has led to some sterling recommendations for her college applications. "Gabriele's always been very social," says her mom, Donna, "but the opportunities Martha presented to her have put her in circles she normally wouldn't have been in. Her involvement with HCI keeps opening doors for her."

Martha also learned some new skills for working with young people—how to push gently without being bossy, how to listen and guide while encouraging someone to try something new and trusting it to work out. "It's never a mistake or a waste of time to reach out to young people," says Martha. "No matter how it happens, whether it's just a nod or a big hug, an hour together eating, or a moment when you ask them if they're okay, it's never a waste of time. You never know the impact you might have."

— *Eighteen-year-old Gabriele, now at college, has added a minor in marketing to her plans to major in sports management. Her favorite sports are field hockey, softball, and track. Martha Grieco has four grown children and has been married to her high school sweetheart for 31 years.*

ALEX GAZCA

The Place Where
Your Spirit Lives

It took three full years to develop the Mercado Central in south Minneapolis, but it only took a short time for the graffiti to start blooming on the walls of local businesses there.

Designed to recreate a traditional Latin American market, the Mercado Central is a member-owned cooperative of Latino businesses. It functions as a commercial and cultural center, with food markets, restaurants, imported art, handicrafts, and music; it also acts as a small business incubator. Fiesta Flor y Diseno, owned by Alex Gazca and his partner, Becky George, is one of the small businesses within the co-op.

Because his flower shop faces the main entrance, Alex often watched people, young and old, coming and going during the day. After businesses had closed for the day, he would sometimes discover graffiti in the bathrooms or outside the building. Instead of calling the police, however, he tried something different—he decided to talk to the kids he thought were doing the damage.

"They were about 14 to 18 years old," says Alex. "They were

these little gang member 'wannabees,' wanting to prove they could be real gang members. One day I said to them, 'I just want to ask you something—why do you do this?' They started being aggressive and I asked one of them if he would let me ask him a personal question. 'Who made your tattoos?' When he told me he had made them himself, I told him they were beautiful and that I thought they were all wasting their talents."

The boys were suddenly intrigued because someone was actually giving them some positive attention. Over the next few weeks, Alex found himself spending more time in conversation and less time cleaning up graffiti.

Alex had emigrated in the early 1980s from Mexico City, where he had been involved in commercial business relations and local politics. He had also been involved in working with youth in his community. In Minneapolis, he wanted to help preserve his cultural traditions, and his activities included serving on the mayor's Latino American advisory group.

In 1997, when Latino graduates of the Neighborhood Development Center's Spanish language training classes recognized a shared need for commercial space, a core group of business owners incorporated as a cooperative, and the Mercado Central was born. Alex got involved in 1998, and the Mercado opened in 1999 with a three-day celebration that attracted 5,000 people. It was in the summer of 2000 that he started talking with the boys in front of his store about how they should feel proud to come to the market. "We want our people to feel like family," Alex told them. "This is a place where the spirit of your country lives."

Alex suggested to these boys that maybe they could start their own businesses, too. "I suggested that maybe we could get them a little table and they could start painting or cartooning, doing caricatures of customers. I said, 'You guys need to think positive, really discover exactly what you like to do the best.'"

Although the boys were too shy to take up some of Alex's suggestions, they appreciated his support and encouragement. Little by little, the boys all started to talk with Alex in a more respectful way and in fact became friendlier with everybody. One boy mentioned he was learning French, and Alex pointed out that the more languages he learned, the more opportunities he created for himself. "Don't waste your time," Alex reiterated. "Work with your ideas in a positive way."

The graffiti problems eventually stopped. Every once in awhile, younger boys will enter the gang, and there might be a few problems. But Alex engages them in conversation, gets to know them, and invites them to get involved in the Mercado in a more positive way.

Why did Alex Gazca decide to talk to these young men instead of just trying to get rid of them? "In my opinion, everyone deserves an opportunity to find out the source of their unhappiness or anger. A lot of these kids don't have anybody to talk to. Many of their parents are coming from very small villages in Mexico, and they both start working when they get here. There's no one to supervise [the kids], and that's when they become attracted to gangs for some attention. If these kids start participating in conversations and meetings, they feel support. They feel like they are safe. No more problems."

— *Alex Gazca became a U.S. citizen in 1998. It was a great day when the business became successful enough to support an employee on the weekends. Alex's children, Daniel and Cristina, help out in the business with everyday tasks as well as wedding and party setups. When asked about his favorite flower, he said it's hard to decide because he feels each one is a work of art.*

*Here, Tenessa Gemelke remembers
how a school counselor gave her a
new image of herself.*

TENESSA GEMELKE

Identity Crisis

〜

As the school year came to a close in the spring of 1990 at Marshall Junior High School in Marshall, Minnesota, all of the 400 students in the 7th and 8th grade were required to attend the annual awards ceremony in the gymnasium. I was finishing my last year there and had gone out of my way to not participate in much or do anything to get noticed, so I figured I was below the radar. I sat quietly while the obvious candidates accepted their awards.

Then Mary Muchlinski, our school counselor, approached the podium to present the biggest award, the Faculty/Staff Award. Faculty members nominated students and then, along with staff, voted to recognize one outstanding boy and one outstanding girl. Typically the winners were above-average students and well liked by their peers, and true to form, the boy who won that year was a good student and fairly popular. As Mrs. Muchlinski began describing the female recipient, it gradually dawned on me that this person sounded a lot like me.

I know junior high can be difficult for everyone, but I was convinced that it was *much worse* for me. I hardly had any friends, boys didn't like me, and my acne was out of control. I was also sure nobody else experienced these things! I was shy and awkward and miserable, and above all, I was sure that adults didn't understand or care about me. The climate at school felt pretty negative to me, and while there were a few exceptional teachers, most seemed to hate their jobs and not care much about students.

I was always an intellectual child, and this caused a real identity crisis for me in junior high school. I went from enjoying spending time at the library and attending math and science camps to an atmosphere where intelligence was now a social deficit. Popularity (whatever that was!) became the only important form of cultural capital. I might as well have had "NERD" written on my forehead in permanent ink. In an act of desperation, I became friends with a girl who hated reading and school in general, but had a winning smile and all the right clothes. I still earned good grades but kept my brains to myself and hoped for the best.

Mrs. Muchlinski was extremely friendly and enthusiastic, but she was certainly not "cool," especially when she tried to get boys and girls mingling at school dances. She seemed to know everybody's name, but I was still surprised the day she stopped me in the hallway early in 8th grade to ask if I would be running for student council. I explained that my popular friend was running, and I didn't want to oppose her. What I didn't say was that I secretly really wanted to be a student council member. I forgot all about this conversation with Mrs. Muchlinski, and I'm sure I rolled my eyes at her several times when I did interact with her during that year.

So there I sat at the awards ceremony, listening to her describe the award-winning student's extracurricular activities on the speech team and school newspaper. I was one of the few girls involved in both those things. She confirmed my suspicions when she told the story about student council. I couldn't believe she even remembered that conversation, much less thought it was important. I'll never forget her final words before announcing my name: "This person stepped aside to support her friend's opportunity to be in student council. Sometimes the best leaders are the ones who encourage leadership in others."

I was stunned by this interpretation. I hadn't realized it, but this woman had been paying attention to me all year. She understood my awkwardness, my love of learning, and my longing to fit in. She stood up in front of the whole school and somehow managed to declare my year of loneliness and shame a success story—an award-winning one! As I walked to the podium that day, I saw my parents. They worked full-time and only rarely attended school events, so Mrs. Muchlinski had obviously gotten them in on the surprise, too. When I returned to sit next to the friend who had served on the student council, she said, "Did you want to be on the student council? It was so nice of you to not run against me!"

As my fellow students congratulated me that day, my self-esteem went through the roof. I had never felt close to Mrs. Muchlinski or considered her one of my favorite adults in the school, but her thoughtful speech that day really changed my whole perspective. I began to recognize my interests in public speaking, reading, and writing as admirable qualities instead of embarrassing flaws. Not only had my teachers validated my participation in these so-called "nerdy" activities, but my peers applauded my success. I entered high school the next year with unexpected confidence and optimism.

I had never really liked Mrs. Muchlinski and always found her questions bothersome and uncomfortable, but despite that, she had persisted, learning quite a bit about me in the process.

Ultimately I was so flattered and grateful that she noticed me. Her speech that day really changed my life.

Now that I'm an adult, I try to remember when I interact with young people that they don't have to *like* me. I have to be secure about myself and accept the fact that they may roll their eyes at me or even reject me, but my efforts can still make a difference. I recall, for example, having a conversation with a 16-year-old boy who was struggling with drugs and in danger of being removed from his home to foster care. We were at a holiday party and he was the only young person there. He certainly didn't appear to be interested in talking to me or anyone else, but I kept asking him questions until I learned that one of his talents was playing the guitar. At a time when he was receiving so many negative messages about being a "bad kid," he was surprised when I complimented him on his interest in music. I took a moment to offer a little support and encouragement even though I was only a peripheral character in his challenging life. It was a brief interaction that may have had no impact on him, but I learned from Mrs. Muchlinski that one caring adult *can* introduce a new outlook into the life of a lonely young person.

— Tenessa Gemelke is an assistant editor at Search Institute. She loves spending time with young people and has worked in neighborhood recreation centers, youth clubs, libraries, and mentoring programs. She's still a nerd and proud of it.

Beyond What You Already Know

—

Sometimes the territory young people need to explore is deep within themselves, but other times, it's outside of them. An adult's role in facilitating that exploration can be as simple as listening to what young people have to say and reflecting back what we've heard, or it can involve actively and specifically pointing out the direction to take. The stories in this section illustrate the lifelong impact a moment's insight or just our simple presence can have in the lives of children and youth.

LEE RUSH

Turning Inward

❧

At 14, Lee Rush faced a problem lots of junior high school students face—who to hang out with. He had come into Pennridge
South Junior High in Perkasie, Pennsylvania, in 1968 with a
clump of friends and was already playing football with a lot
of them, but he soon found himself drawn to another group, a
tougher crowd that was more in the fast lane. Sometimes when
he hung around with these guys, he did things he knew he wasn't
supposed to. For a while, he did those things without getting
caught.

One day in the school cafeteria, a food fight broke out. Lee
skirted the edges of it for quite a while, but finally decided to
throw something just for the heck of it. He felt a hand clamp
down on his shoulder, and he turned to look into the face of his
football coach, Willis Frank. But instead of sending Lee down to
the office, Coach Frank asked the boy to walk with him down to
his classroom. The two sat and talked for a few minutes before
the coach made his point.

"I've been watching you for the last couple of months," the
coach said. "I've noticed you've been starting to hang around

with a different group of kids lately. I'd like you to think about something. Do you like yourself? Do you really like the man you're becoming?"

Lee recalls that the entire conversation lasted less than 10 minutes. The coach didn't send him to the office or give him a detention. The coach just asked him to consider his question and get back to him with an answer when he had one. Lee doesn't remember that they ever had another conversation specifically about the incident, but Lee did start thinking. It turned out that he wasn't really happy with himself.

"The seed was planted," reflects Lee. "He didn't lecture or make a statement about what he thought was right or wrong. He just asked the right question at the right time that helped turn me inward. By sharing his experience, he exercised a really powerful intervention without using his power or authority."

Lee eventually decided to change peer groups, and once he started leaving the more troublesome group, he encouraged some friends to do the same. He so angered the leader of that group, in fact, that one day at the local pool hall, the group leader punched Lee in the face and knocked him to the ground, warning Lee to stop talking about him.

Within twenty years after this incident, Lee says, half of the kids in that tough crowd were either dead or in prison. "It took a lot of courage to leave that crowd. I could have gone either way. The coach's question was definitely a marker in time that got me thinking about what I was doing."

Years later when he became a youth counselor for kids coming out of juvenile court, Lee found it especially ironic that the new alternative high school he started work in was that pool hall-turned-store front.

Eventually Lee went on to train counselors as well, often telling the story of Coach Frank's intervention to remind people that you never know what you say to young people that will make a difference. "It's like watching one of those little clear piggybanks where you can see the tumblers on the combination lock sliding back and forth into place. You may never know which intervention or which question you use that will turn that last tumbler. It's not your job to try and figure out if a young person is listening or not, it's just your job to pose the good questions."

— *Lee Rush is executive director of justCommunity, Inc., in Quakertown, Pennsylvania, a nonprofit that works in community mobilization, restorative justice, and youth development. He is also the coordinator for the Healthy Communities • Healthy Youth of Upper Bucks initiative. Lee lives with his wife, Kathy, and 10-year-old daughter, Sage, who has reignited Lee's love for baseball.*

A Stunning Thought

~

Nothing seemed out of the ordinary as 17-year-old Nancy Ashley made her way to her final appointment with her high school guidance counselor, Jane Hackbardt. It was the spring of 1970, and in a few months, Nancy would leave her tiny hometown of Howard City, Michigan, to attend Central Michigan University. College life would still be relatively protected, but for Nancy, growing up in a community where she knew every one of the town's 600 residents as neighbors, it was going to be like stepping out on Broadway.

While coping with the isolation of small-town life, Nancy had also struggled with the impact of her father's alcoholism and abuse on her family. Going away to college would be an escape of sorts for Nancy, even though most young women in her community had been led to believe that they really only had two choices about what to pursue in college—nursing or teaching. "I hated blood," says Nancy, "so I sure wasn't going to be a nurse."

Nancy sat down in Jane's small, windowless office. Nevertheless, the tiny room had a brightness to it because of the little touches that were emblematic of Jane's spunky personality. Jane had a reputation for cheerleading her students, but even that didn't prepare Nancy for what Jane Hackbardt said that day. "I clearly remember her telling me that there was a whole big world out there," recalls Nancy. "'When you get to college,' she said, 'look around. You have more choices. You don't have to follow a path that's not right for you.' That was such a stunning thought to me, I just couldn't get it out of my head."

Nancy pursued college like a starving person suddenly seated at the banquet table, changing majors four times as she sampled subjects as diverse as French and economics. She carried Jane's words with her as she went out into the wide world after graduating with a degree in office administration and settled in Lansing to work. A law school opened that students could attend at night, and some of Nancy's friends started going. "I truly think I always had a little social justice flame burning because of what happened in my family," says Nancy, "but it never occurred to me that I could go to law school. Nobody in our town ever did that." Nancy successfully passed the entrance exam and told herself she'd try just one session to see how she liked it. She was hooked.

Nancy got her law degree and handled divorces, wills, and business litigation for a decade before once again hearing Jane's words about choice ringing in her head. Casting about for the next bend in her path, Nancy realized that her passion lay in the areas in which she'd been volunteering for many years—domestic violence, children, youth, and families. She decided to put her talents, experiences, skills, and passions to work in strategic and policy planning where, to this day, Nancy jokes, "I very rarely use French."

Nancy now runs her own company, Heliotrope, which provides planning services for clients in child care, out-of-school time care, domestic violence, juvenile justice, youth development, and community development. Nancy and her associate, Christina Malecka, have helped shape community-improvement initiatives in the Puget Sound area, including Seattle's It's About Time for Kids asset initiative, King County's Making Connections neighborhood initiative under the aegis of the Annie E. Casey Foundation, and the SafeFutures juvenile crime reduction initiative. Nancy also crafted the first template for a state-of-the-art domestic violence response system as part of a national movement to develop Domestic Violence Coordinated Response Systems.

Once introduced to asset building, Nancy took steps to deliberately embed the Developmental Assets framework in every aspect of her business as well as her personal approach to supporting children and families. In 2001, for example, Nancy volunteered to be a Big Sister, eventually stepping in to become a strong advocate for her little sister when the girl's home life suddenly deteriorated. At one point, Nancy and her husband, Fred Bird, who don't have children of their own, had one hour to decide if they could take in the 13-year-old girl and her 11-year-old brother rather than send the children to foster care. What was supposed to be a short-term solution stretched into nearly a year of unexpected parenting as the courts sorted out the best solution for the family.

Jane's earlier advice has helped Nancy professionally as well as personally when she was deciding to become a Big Sister and foster parent to two children. "I've often used what Jane told me. I've been able to act on my own instincts rather than other people's ideas of what they think is the 'right' choice for me. Jane's advice reminds me that I have choices even if I don't know what they are at the moment," says Nancy. "She noticed me and the dilemma I was in. By seizing that moment, she made a huge difference in the paths I've taken."

Nancy had occasion some years ago to return to Howard

City and to tell Jane Hackbardt about the difference she'd made in one girl's life. "I now know she wished someone had said that to her. She was a little out of the box in Howard City and had to forge her own way. I think she was passing on something that she had yearned for and realized others needed to hear. She knew exactly what she was doing."

— *Nancy Ashley founded Heliotrope to seed positive change in the community through planning, consultation, and coaching. She lives in Seattle, Washington, with her husband, Fred Bird, and two highly skilled feline entertainers named Rosa and Marshmallow.*

Action as Opportunity

At 14, Kevin Dilmore was a "normal" kid, growing up in the seventies in Abilene, Kansas. His parents had divorced when he was younger, but his mom was happily remarried to a municipal court judge, and Kevin and his younger sister had a good life in a small town of 6,000. Kevin watched TV, indulged in humorous satire, and was a regular fixture at the local library.

It was in English class at Abilene High School during Kevin's freshman year that he met teacher Tom Kite—and just at the right time, according to Kevin. "I was rapidly becoming one of those smart-ass kids who would rather buck the system than work within it," recalls Kevin. "But Tom was the person who encouraged me to take my creative angst and make it constructive."

Kite was 33 at the time, about the same size as most of his students, with a quick smile and big laugh. He had a few hard-and-fast rules in the classroom, but mostly won students' cooperation through his ability to get them to take risks and be creative. In addition to teaching English, he was also the high school's wrestling coach and yearbook advisor. Kevin found himself becoming a part of a very tight group of young people working on the yearbook, all closely bonded to Kite.

Tom Kite's particular gift was for taking the time to connect with his students one-on-one, especially if he heard any rumblings about potential problems. The year a 15-year-old student's mom committed suicide, Kite made sure the young woman stayed connected at school even as she assumed some of the responsibilities for her family's household.

Kite also used his skills for assessing a student's creative interests and doled out assignments in line with those interests. He found short-story contests for Kevin to enter, and as Kevin became enamored of *Saturday Night Live* during high school, Kite had him writing SNL-style skits to promote yearbook sales at rallies. When the junior-class play was cancelled for lack of interest, Kite let Kevin fill the two pages in the yearbook that would have been devoted to the play with an essay on what happens to morale when there's no participation. "He was always finding ways for us to be creative and effect change in the system instead of lobbing rocks toward it. He also found ways for me personally to follow my predilections toward satire and parody while making sure I didn't get myself in trouble."

Kevin's personal turning point came in 1982 when his idol, John Belushi, died from a drug overdose. "I had been oblivious to what was going on in his outside life," says Kevin. "I was devastated." Kevin came to school the Monday after the news broke with a giant poster of Belushi, which he proceeded, without permission, to hang on the wall in Tom Kite's classroom. Kite was savvy enough to see Kevin's action as an opportunity. Without comment, the poster was left on the wall the entire year.

"I asked him about it later," says Kevin. "He said he chose to leave it up because he figured it was my outlet for mourning a teen idol, but we also had some conversations then about how Belushi had become a victim of success and squandered his gifts for performing."

What Kevin learned from Tom was how to mold his creativity into a tool for change. "He encouraged me to be a person who drafts a proposal to a superior at work in hopes of improving a situation rather than a person who gripes around the water cooler." Using storytelling as his vehicle, Kevin earned two separate degrees in college, a BA in film studies and a BS in journalism, then spent a number of years as the cops and court reporter for the *Miami County Republic* in Paola, Kansas. Kevin is now a science fiction writer, producing short stories and novels with his writing partner, Dayton Ward.

He lost track of Kite for a number of years until his phone rang at home one day after he'd been writing features for the *Star Trek Communicator* for about a year. "Is this Kevin Dilmore? The same guy who writes for the official *Star Trek* magazine?" Instantly recognizing his voice, Kevin shot back, "Is this the guy who encouraged him to write?" Kite, it turned out, was a fellow *Trek* fan and subscriber, thrilled to see his former student published in the magazine.

"I wasn't a kid in crisis," says Kevin, "but I could well have sat back, being critical, not doing anything. Tom was the guy who most convincingly pointed out to me that you can let your ideas fester or you can step forward with a better way to express yourself. Those lessons of speaking for yourself and expressing yourself constructively came at a critical time, and I now share them with my daughters. I hope those lessons improve their dealings with people on the playground as well as in the classroom."

— *Kevin Dilmore writes science fiction from Prairie Village, Kansas, with the support of his wife, Michelle, and daughters, 14-year-old Stacy and 10-year-olds Colleen and Amy. He can still recite all of the dialogue from* Animal House.

A Quiet Spirit

Alfonso Wyatt has never been sure how it came about, but when he was 22 years old, growing up in Queens, New York, it somehow fell to him to drive a family friend to dialysis three times a week. The Reverend Rudolph Boone had been a friend of the Wyatt family for many years, serving as pastor of the Jon Hus Moravian Church they attended. Alfonso didn't know it at the time, but Reverend Boone, a handsome, pipe-smoking man in his 50s with a full head of gray hair, was dying of renal failure.

The young man had just graduated from Howard University in Washington, D.C., and was trying to figure out what to do with his life. "I had my own fears and concerns," recalls Alfonso. "I was trying to figure out what kind of man I wanted to be, and at that age, the jury's still out. I knew I had to make some concrete decisions. I had to start facing up to some facts. It was 1972, and the country was still dealing with the impact of Vietnam. I would be leaving home soon, probably getting married in a few years. But I had not yet decided how I was going to live."

Alfonso tried to accomplish gracefully this unwanted task he had been given. One silver lining was the fact that he got to drive the Reverend's car—a hot, hunter green Camaro. While the elder man was enduring his treatments, Alfonso had a few hours to drive around the neighborhood in this snazzy muscle car.

For each treatment, Alfonso would walk the three blocks from his house to Reverend Boone's, and from there they made the 20-minute drive out to Long Island City. Long Island City had been known during WWII for having more factories per square mile than any other place in America. Driving out to the dialysis center on cold winter nights, past dark, hulking factories closed for the day, passing underneath elevated trains, produced a sense of foreboding in Alfonso. "Being there at night with all those old factories closed felt like being at death's door," he remembers. Despite the fact that he had a reputation among his friends and family for habitually running late, he was never late to pick up Reverend Boone when his treatments were done. "I'd wait for him, and he would come back out in slow, measured steps. I knew I could never hang him up."

But what Alfonso most remembers now is that over the course of many weeks driving back and forth to dialysis, the two men had conversation. A lot of conversation. "I started thinking about things to ask him. Even in his suffering, he was gentle and never bitter. He was the kindest man I ever met, and in the three or four months before he died, I grew to love him and the time we were able to spend together. I couldn't tell you about any particular conversation we had. It was the total impact of the experience, being able to hear his wisdom, to see what dignity looks like. He was able to show me how to live, what to say, and to bring those two things as close together as possible for me. He was a quiet spirit that I wanted to honor."

Alfonso was about to enter graduate school, although he had not yet made a decision about his future career. Because his father was a minister, he had deliberately looked at other options.

But eventually the impact of his conversations with Reverend Boone shifted him into that very direction. "I believe that God planted a seed, and I willingly allowed myself to be opened to the idea of going into the ministry. Because of Reverend Boone, I learned the power of one. I know he was just being himself, and because of the circumstances, it would have been easy for me at that dumb age to see something other than what was real. But it was a real-life moment and I shared it with another human being."

The impact of that sharing continues, he says. "Now when I'm out speaking with people, I always ask them to think of that one person in their lives, outside their family, who made a difference to them."

— *Alfonso Wyatt is an associate minister at the Greater Allen Cathedral of New York, an African/Methodist/Episcopal church started by runaway American slaves. He and his wife, Ouida, have been married for 30 years, and although they have no biological children, Alfonso says hundreds of children (and some adults!) call him Uncle Fonso. He is about to publish his first book,* Mad Truth: Lessons for Students of Life, *and his wife sometimes lets him drive her new Mercedes.*

*Marin Orlosky describes how
the confidence of an encouraging
dance instructor gave her
confidence in herself.*

MARIN ORLOSKY

Just Go

—

"Just go," she said. I stared at the paper Nancy Warner, the director of Pennington Dance in my New Jersey hometown, threw at me, announcing an upcoming master class with ballet star Suzanne Farrel. "But it says you have to be at least 16," I stammered, "and I'm only 14. And it's in a city an hour away. And it says you need a minimum of four years experience on pointe and I've only had—"

Nancy clasped my hand. "I know what it says. Go anyway. Trust me. You can handle it." She left me standing outside the studio, mouth agape. For the first time, someone had enough faith in my abilities to tell me to seek opportunities beyond my community.

Even though neither of my parents were performers or artists, they had always encouraged my brother and me to pursue activities we enjoyed. But they were also realistic in their view of how competitive the dance world is. I had not mentioned to Nancy my recent desire to intensify my dance training in preparation for a professional dance career, but she must have seen the passion behind the attentiveness with which I awaited each audition for local performances.

She must also have overheard me pleading unsuccessfully with my parents to let me take classes at the only larger dance school in our area, whose teaching philosophy they disagreed with. Yet here was a new option. Nancy had suddenly opened my eyes to a whole new range of possibilities.

I didn't wind up going to that master class in 1999 (it was in the morning and my parents believed school was more important), but Nancy's words changed my life. From that time on, my parents realized I could hold my own in more professional-level classes, and I constantly capitalized on opportunities outside the familiar. I soon began exploring public transportation, taking the train to my newfound dance classes in New York City. I tried long-distance swimming and swam four miles in one afternoon. My best friend offered me voice lessons, and I wound up with a solo in chorus one year. I also started befriending adults, discovering the fascinating opinions and life stories of my teachers, neighbors, fellow dancers, homeless people, and nursing home residents.

At first I was terrified of all these new activities, but I soon learned I could hold my own in both high-level dance classes and conversations with people on the other side of the generation gap. As my self-confidence grew, so did my relationships with adults. I discussed art with the mother of a younger dancer at the studio. A homeless man confided in me his songwriting aspirations. An elderly tap dancer regaled me weekly with tales of her glory days dancing with Fred Astaire and Leslie Caron.

Because of Nancy's encouragement to look beyond what I know well, I now welcome new experiences wholeheartedly. From delivering groceries to residents of low-income urban housing with the Crisis Ministry of Princeton to striking up conversations with fellow riders on New Jersey Transit to trying hip-hop dance classes, every situation where I would have previously felt out of place has brought me immeasurable rewards. As a result of Nancy Warner's guidance, this unfamiliar terrain is exciting instead of scary, and I can't wait to discover what awaits me if I "just go."

← *Marin Orlosky has been involved with her local Healthy Communities • Healthy Youth initiative since 1999, including presenting an intergenerational workshop on Developmental Assets in the arts with fellow students and her mother, Judy. Marin, now 19 years old, has danced with numerous prestigious schools and companies and currently choreographs and performs with the Harvard-Radcliff Dance Company and Harvard Ballet Company while she attends Harvard University.*

Unhistoric Acts

~

In his book about St. Louis Park's Children First Initiative in Minnesota, Robert Ramsey tells the story shared by food service employee Delores Therres at her retirement. She remembered leaving her ticket room one day as a young girl came running down the hall toward her—she was late. Delores told her, "Honey, don't run. I'll wait for you." The girl started to cry. When Delores asked why, the girl said, "Nobody's ever called me 'honey' before, not even my mother." Delores put her arm around the girl, gave her a big hug, and then went back to her office and had a good cry. "Vignettes like this," wrote Ramsey, "are powerful reminders that the best of Children First is often made up of unhistoric acts performed by unlikely heroes." Most of us don't set out to be heroes in the lives of children, but as the stories in this section will reveal, heroes are often made in small ways.

CHRISTINA BARRY AND
DAPHNE SCHROTH

Just All the Little Things

Daphne Schroth used to watch those television spots where they would highlight a child who needs to be adopted and think maybe she could give something to a child who didn't have very much. An "Air Force brat," she'd grown up in a big family, traveling and living all over the world. Her own children were grown, but she still wanted to have a young child in her life. When she moved from Milwaukee to Frisco, Colorado, in 1993, she worked in an office building shared by the Mountain Mentor program. After watching them operate for about six months, she liked what she saw. So she walked down the hall and told them she wanted to get involved.

She had no idea how two lives were about to be changed.

The first time she saw Christina Barry, the child she would mentor, the little girl was just finishing 4th grade. Daphne had been told that the child was coming from difficult circumstances, transitioning from foster care almost at birth to the reluctant care of her grandmother at age 3. "When I first met Christina, her grandmother was working second shift, so she was alone from after school until 11 PM at night," says Daphne. "Christina had few social skills, had never had her hair cut in a shop, or even gone shopping for clothes in a store. Her academic record was poor, and I remember a school counselor telling me he didn't think she'd make it to 7th grade."

But there was a spark in Christina that Daphne saw right away. "She was the most joyful, delightful child who appreciated everything. I remember the first time my husband and I took her to lunch, not realizing that her experiences weren't like my kids' experiences. I asked if she liked Chinese food, and she said yes, but I don't think she'd ever had it before. We went to a buffet, and she just kept going back and back. My husband and I couldn't believe that skinny little girl could eat so much!"

Christina had had other mentors before. "Most of the mentors I'd met were supposed to spend time with you a few hours a week," says Christina, "but after a short time, many of them moved away or found better things to do. Daphne and I hit it off right away and started hanging out a lot. She really liked me, and we started doing all the fun activities that kids normally do that I'd never done before. We'd go to her house and plan really fun things, go to the movies, go bike riding. I knew how to swim, but Daphne actually helped me with diving and strokes and stuff."

Daphne loves sports, and she quickly saw Christina's interest in swimming as a way to get her involved in a number of things. "One motivation was just to get her in the shower three times a week!" says Daphne. "I gave her a big bottle of shampoo and said, 'This is yours.'" A few years later, swimming provided another important outlet. "When Christina was 14, she started working at a local A&W. Some of the older kids were providing alcohol and drugs to the younger kids, but I came across a program where the local recreation center would pay kids to train as lifeguards if they stayed on. So I helped Christina get trained at age 15, and by the time she was 16, she was on staff." Christina now works as a lifeguard and swim instructor while she's putting herself through college.

While the two women have forged a deep bond in the last decade, there were some rough spots along the way. "I hardly ever get sick," says Daphne, "but one winter I got bronchitis. Our contract said we would get together for at least three hours a week, but during one two-week stretch, I couldn't see her at all. Finally I picked her up for a sleigh ride we were going to take, and she wouldn't talk to me. I asked her, 'What's up?' She said, 'We have a contract and you owe me six hours!'"

That comment made it clear to both of them how important the relationship was becoming. "I was home alone a lot and didn't have a good relationship with my grandmother," says Christina. "She had to work a lot, but she also wasn't very supportive of my relationship with Daphne. At times I was verbally and even physically abused. It was hard, and for a really long time I just wanted to go home with Daphne, but I couldn't. I was mad sometimes, but I was young."

The relationship helped Christina reach a turning point in her junior year of high school. "She seemed to have an especially tough time in the years leading up to that," says Daphne. "Her home situation got so bad in 9th grade, she was put in foster care again, but then she just seemed to really figure out what she was going to have to do to live."

"I was beginning to realize that I'd be 18 soon, and I'd have to move out and live on my own," recalls Christina of that critical year. "Daphne talked to me about college, and I began to realize that it could be a reality for me. I started working as a lifeguard 20 hours a week to save money for college and a car. I also met my future fiancé around that time, and he was a good motivator."

Their fondest memory? A trip to Paris they took together when Christina graduated from high school. Christina had studied French for six years, and the school planned a spring trip to France that Daphne thought was outrageously expensive and Christina knew she'd never be able to afford. "Daphne asked me one night at dinner about the trip in a way that made me think she wasn't interested in it, but that winter she surprised me by saying we'd better start getting ready. I was jumping up and down. I'd never even been on an airplane."

The trip worked out beautifully for the neophyte traveler. "She was the most delightful traveling partner," says Daphne. "I remember her standing in front of great works of art, unable to tear herself away. Here was this young woman who had had so many hardships and never complained. She really appreciates life, and she has enhanced mine so much."

The trip was a milestone, but it is the impact of the overall relationship that has been the most important for both of them. "When I was younger, I would sometimes feel really bad about how I was dressed," says Christina. "I didn't have what other kids had. Daphne just always made sure I didn't feel out of place. Sometimes it was something as simple as making sure I had school supplies, or she'd come and watch me in activities in middle school to cheer me on so I wouldn't feel like the only one without a person there. If I hadn't had her guidance and help, I don't think I would have done as much as I've done so far."

Christina is now in her second year of college at Metro State in Denver, Colorado, studying business and finance with an eye on getting her degree and then a real estate license. "I wouldn't have gone to college without Daphne," says Christina. "She advised me, helped me set up meetings with counselors, pick a school, get scholarships. She really encouraged me and advised me on a lot of things."

"I believe in mentoring," says Daphne. "If a child can have one positive adult role model in their life, it can make a huge difference."

➙ Daphne Schroth is Human Services Director for Summit County in Frisco, Colorado. Her nickname is "Frog" because she has trouble sitting still, and she's married to a wonderful man who keeps up on all her adventures. Her daughter, Kristi, is a physician, and her son, Geoff, is an improv actor in Chicago. Christina Barry, a "great shopper" and an animal lover, is attending Metro State College in Denver. The children and adults she teaches in swimming and aerobics like her and think she's funny. She recently found a previously unknown cousin from her father's family through an Internet search.

PAUL STAPLETON AND
MIKE CUMNOCK

Permanent Grandparents

No way was Paul Stapleton going to clean his room. They couldn't do anything to him that hadn't already been done. At the ripe old age of 8, Paul had already been expelled from school lots of times, gotten in plenty of fights, run away from home repeatedly, and been in 11 institutions including a psychiatric hospital. He was tougher than those guys at the Ranch.

But a little part of Paul began to think cleaning his room wasn't such a bad thing. Maybe he could talk to Mike about it. Paul had met Mike Cumnock in 1992, when he was first admitted to the Arkansas Sheriff's Youth Ranch in Batesville. Neither his parents nor his aunt could handle him. The Ranch was the only place left that would take him. Paul hadn't trusted anyone enough for a long time to even want a relationship, let alone have one, but Paul understood instinctively that something was different about Mike. "It was his personality and his heart," says Paul. "He's someone you could trust. He would tell me I'd done a good job when others wouldn't. He'd give me attention whether I did the job or not, but I got more if I did, and I wanted his attention. He made things seem okay."

Even now, at age 20 and attending college in Washington state, Paul has a special bond with Mike. "He was the person I went to to sort out problems. He came and sat with me that day and stayed with me the whole time I was cleaning my room. I cleaned it for him."

Paul is one of Mike's special success stories, but thanks to the Ranch, he is one of many. Conceived as a safety net for abused and troubled children with no other place to go, the Ranch has five campuses around the state. The Ranch takes little or no federal or state funding, with most of its support coming from small, grassroots donations from each and every one of the state's 75 counties. Besides offering a stable home, the Ranch helps kids heal from broken lives, especially through working with animals and riding horses.

"We set ourselves apart to take the kids with the greatest need and least resources," says Mike, CEO of the Ranch. "For failed adoptions, for kids who say they can't stand to go to another foster home. They complete their own application to be admitted here, and once they come here, they can live here as long as they want." Unlike many programs that terminate their involvement when a child reaches 18, the Ranch will support a young person for as long as he or she wants the support, providing a place to live or as much financial support for college as possible.

Mike likes to think of his program as "permanent grandparents." "My own grandparents were always there for me," says Mike of Herman and Clara Cumnock, who lived in downtown Little Rock. "My parents had a troubled relationship and eventually divorced. At one point, my grandparents invited me to move in with them, which I did."

Herman was a mechanical engineer with a good job, but not a lot of money. Mike remembers that lack of money didn't make much of a difference. Mostly he remembers piling into a station wagon with 14 other family members to spend an afternoon wading in the local creek. Or Clara out picking up bottles on the side of the road to raise money for the church. "My grandparents were just common sense," says Mike. "I live my life in a lot of ways just like them."

Mike works hard to emulate personally and through the Ranch what his grandparents gave him—lots of freedom, but with clear boundaries and always being there for the long haul. Paul definitely feels he benefited from the legacy that Mike's grandparents passed down. "The ranch was a good place to grow up," says Paul. "Mike gave me a light at the end of the tunnel. He seemed sincerely concerned about me. Not just what I was doing, but what was wrong with me and why I was getting into so much trouble."

One of the things Mike helped figure out was that Paul was suffering from a seizure disorder. A lot of his worst behavior— skateboarding off the roof or even attacking people—occurred during seizure blackouts, leaving Paul with no memory of what had happened. Once the right medication was prescribed, many of those problems disappeared, and Paul was finally able to make some progress. He tried living with his parents again at about age 13, leaving the Ranch after five years to join them in Seattle, but it didn't work out. Paul got involved with gangs and drugs for a time, ending up in juvenile detention and later a group home. He kept up contact with Mike, though, sometimes calling drunk from the street. The connection got really thin for a while, but he knew Mike still cared about him. Paul finally decided to get his life back.

"I had changed, but my parents had not," says Paul of his personal turning point several years ago. "I realized I was going to live on this earth a few more years whether I wanted to or not. I had a girlfriend who had been with me since I was 14, and she helped me straighten up, too."

Occasionally seeking long-distance advice from Mike, Paul got into an accelerated career-training program with the Job Corps and has been attending Skagit Valley Community College. He plans to get a master's degree in hotel management and administration with an eye toward eventually investing in real estate.

"If I had to say anything about Mike," says Paul, "I'd say he was like my grandfather. Whenever I got into trouble, I'd run to him. I had been so damaged as a little kid that there were times I hated being at the Ranch, but I realize now they gave me so many opportunities."

Paul is poised to embark on a new adventure in his life, returning to Batesville to continue college. His partner, Melody, is going with him. Part of what gives him the courage to make such a transition is what he's learned about relationships from Mike. "Over a period of about seven years, I didn't have much contact with Mike, but I learned that there was still a friendship there, there's something to hold on to. You can have relationships that last. Even though I'm leaving friends behind in Washington, I know now I can still have that same thing."

"Everyone has the opportunity to shape children's lives," says Mike. "Some of us make it a career, and for others it can be as simple as teaching Sunday school or thanking the sacker at the grocery store."

— *Paul has done so well academically in college that he was nominated as one of* USA Today's *national academic all-stars. Mike and his wife, Sarah, have been married for 34 years and, in addition to raising their daughter, Mara, have been foster parents to 13 other children. Mike says both he and Paul consider themselves examples of "beating the odds."*

RACHEL

The Longest Journey

~

For Rachel, there is no single superhero who changed her life; rather, she experienced a series of adults who made it possible for her to construct a happy, successful life for herself, despite the difficulty of that journey.

The 22-year-old woman, who prefers to use only her first name, was born in Ethiopia, East Africa. The earliest caregiver she remembers is her grandmother, who took her in after her teenaged mother abandoned her on a park bench when she was very young. Her father had already left for America to escape the Ethiopian military. He tried unsuccessfully for many years to bring Rachel and her older sister to live with him, but despite the fact that her mother had abandoned the children, she wouldn't sign the papers to release them into their father's custody.

Rachel remembers her grandmother as being "everything." "She made me feel that she cared about me 100 percent," says Rachel. "She worked hard and did everything for me and my sister from the time she got up in the morning until she said her prayers at night. She gave so much."

The struggle to raise two little girls in near-poverty took its toll on her grandmother, though, and Rachel was sent to live with other family members at age 3. Rachel's father sent money for two years to an uncle to help pay for his daughters' care until he found out that the uncle was keeping the money for himself. Rachel was allowed to go back to living with her grandmother, but only until her father could bring the girls to the United States.

Rachel was only 10 years old that day in 1992 when she and her sister were put on an airplane alone to fly to Pennsylvania to meet her father. "I was very excited," Rachel recalls. "I thought it would be cool, but I also thought we were just going for a two-week vacation. I desperately wanted to go back to my grandmother, but everyone kept telling us how lucky we were, so I didn't feel like I could be ungrateful or cry about missing my grandmother."

The promise of Rachel's new life in this country quickly dissipated as her new stepmother put her and her sister to work taking care of little brothers and sisters. Moving was traumatic enough, but trying to navigate public education and English-as-a-Second-Language classes was very difficult, too. The family ended up moving to Atlanta. Rachel's father, unfortunately, became an abusive, manipulative man who used mental and physical abuse to try to control his outspoken daughter. At 16, Rachel got up the courage to tell a high school counselor she was being abused at home. The state intervened immediately, and Rachel never went home again. Her sister dropped out of school soon after, and to this day, Rachel doesn't know where she is.

Rachel found herself living in Elks Aidmore Children's Center in Conyers, Georgia, a shelter for children, while finishing high school. The center had a mentoring program through which Rachel was introduced to Jeannie and Clark Hinkel, who would become her foster parents by the time Rachel started college. "It was really, really hard to trust anyone completely," says Rachel. "I wanted a family, but I wasn't ready for it and wasn't looking for one at that time. It was hard for them because I'm Ethiopian and they're southern Whites, but even though we were different, we didn't see each other like that."

Living with the Hinkels, Rachel was able to rediscover the simple joys of daily living within a family—having meals together, going to church, being encouraged to explore and develop her interests.

The safety of having a loving home, coupled with an opportunity to see a therapist, allowed Rachel to touch something that had been buried deep inside her since she was small—her love of art. "I used to make art back in 3rd grade, but my father was so discouraging that I stopped doing it until my senior year of high school. It started out as an escape, a hobby, but then it became more than that."

As she contemplated college, Rachel decided to study art. She now attends the Savannah College of Arts and Design on a full scholarship with a double major in painting and photography and a minor in printmaking. She is starting to become known in her community not only for her riveting work, but also for the fact that the young artist declines to sell her work directly. Instead, Rachel donates her work to be sold for charitable causes such as raising money for the local rape crisis center.

Rachel says embracing her art has healed her in many ways. "My sister and I didn't have a whole lot when we were in Ethiopia. My sister and I would sometimes have five cents between us, and we were happy. Then we went to live with my father, where we had everything that's supposed to make you happy, like clothes. I've had nothing, and I've had everything, but now I know what makes me happy—art. I want to help out, to give

100 percent, and what better way to do that? Because I feel as if I give 100 percent in my artwork."

Rachel credits one of her professors, Richard Gere (no relation to the actor), with also providing her extraordinary support in school, but it's to the Hinkels that Rachel goes for the holidays. "They are amazing and loving. The fact that they could take me in and treat me like one of their own is surprising to this day. I'd never felt really comfortable anywhere, but they have given me so much. I know they'd do anything for me, and I would do anything for them."

— *Rachel is the founder of Artists for Charity, a group dedicated to supporting various causes worldwide, and was a National Foster Care Award winner in 2003. Her latest project is organizing a group show with other students at her college to raise money to pay for health insurance for uninsured students.*

NANCY SLACK

Building Relationships, One Pancake at a Time

Making pancakes for 25 middle school children every Friday morning before school was not something Nancy Slack ever deliberately thought about doing. She didn't set out to cook hundreds of pancakes as her son John and his friends made their way through grades 6 to 8 in their suburban neighborhood. When she was done, however, she had given—and received—a lot more than she ever imagined.

It all started because John wasn't quite ready for school one morning. The Slack family was new to their Portland, Oregon, community, and the middle school was only three blocks from their house. John's new buddies would swing by his house to pick him up every morning for the short walk to school. Sometimes John's friends would show up early before John was dressed, or John just wasn't quite together to walk out the door. Nancy asked one morning if the kids had had breakfast, and that's when she fired up the griddle. One Friday morning, she invited John's friends to plan on having breakfast, and the next thing she knew, she was cooking pancakes every Friday morning. As more young people got wind of things, a few more started showing up.

"I'd flip pancakes and pour juice," says Nancy. "They'd just forget I was there, listening in. I'd just stand there with a smile on my face. It was such an easy way to get to know these kids."

Nancy made pancakes through the 7th grade when girls started to join the group and the dynamics changed. She flipped pancakes the day after one of the school's administrators—the designated disciplinarian, in fact—was publicly arrested for selling pot. She listened through the conversations when the students' favorite guidance counselor was hurt in a serious car accident. "The pancakes were only the focus for a few of the kids who started their growth spurts and wanted to eat. For most of them, it was about getting together and talking. As a result, I learned a lot about my son and had incredible relationships with these kids. I haven't made pancakes in three years, but there are young people at the high school who still greet me as 'Mom' as I walk down the hall."

By the time John and his friends started 8th grade, Friday morning breakfast included a minimum of a dozen young people, and Nancy found herself making pancakes for as many as 25. She always kept things informal, letting kids know they were always welcome and making sure she had enough food for whoever might come. The front hall was a mountain of backpacks, and the kitchen was a train wreck afterwards, but through it all, Nancy learned that just by being present, you can be a positive influence on your own children and their friends.

"It's really important to show kids they can have adults in their lives that they can talk to. I think it's important to just be available to them, to sit back and let them have a good time and not butt in. I just listened to their opinions and only offered mine if they asked for it. I was there, and I'm still there for them."

— Nancy Slack lives with her family in Portland and is regional director for Destination Imagination, a program that builds Developmental Assets through team building and creative problem solving. She is a freelance writer and consultant to nonprofit organizations.

Brent Bolstrom recalls how his
intentional efforts to be attentive
helped one little girl thrive.

BRENT BOLSTROM

What I Knew about Zora

On a brisk fall afternoon in 2001, I watched children play in
the yard at a treatment facility for children with emotional and
behavioral difficulties where I had been working for only a few
months. I thought to myself about how their backgrounds were
sadly too similar—broken homes, abusive caregivers, long stints
in foster care, and histories of neglect inconceivable to most
outside this line of work.

I enjoyed my job as a primary care counselor, but the stress
was beginning to take a toll on my ability to provide an effective
therapeutic environment for these kids. The small group exer-
cises I ran were in complete disarray. The children's van rides to
and from school consisted of daily screaming matches (and a few
thrown punches) over which seat was best or where to tune the
radio. Cooperative games weren't so cooperative.

Yet on this day, I watched as one of my co-workers, Michelle,
managed her group with apparent ease and delight. These kids
enjoyed the careless play of childhood—made friends, tiptoed

toward their independence, but also worked together and developed their sense of self.

So how did she do it? I realized that Michelle had the foundational quality often referred to in parenting manuals or research literature I had come across—the ability to masterfully maintain the delicate balance between discipline and warmth. She provided a structured environment characterized by consistent messages and boundaries. But more importantly, she was also very intentional about getting to know personal items about each and every child she worked with, such as what they enjoyed playing, where they went to school, how they liked their food, and the kinds of music they listened to.

It was amazing to watch children's eyes light up when they would notice that Michelle thought enough about them to be interested in and to talk to them about their daily lives. They responded to her curiosity with a degree of respect and openness I seldom witnessed with the children I worked with over this short period of time. I figured it couldn't hurt to try some of these techniques since nothing else had appeared to work for me. I decided to start with Zora (not her real name).

Zora was a beautiful 10-year-old child who had had a really rough life. Abused and abandoned by her biological parents, Zora had difficulty staying in a stable foster family due to her verbal and physical aggression toward others. Most of the time she sat alone and rarely talked. This quietness was deceiving, however, as she could quickly turn any routine classroom exercise into all-out chaos among her classmates. Because she felt abandoned in the past, she was particularly reluctant to make a connection with any adult in her life for fear of being let down or forgotten about, and acting out was her way of sustaining this disconnect. There were two things I knew about Zora: (1) she was a phenomenal artist full of boundless creativity, and (2) she was very proud of the new hairstyles that her foster sister made up for her each morning.

I began by asking Zora how she felt about drawing some pictures of me for my apartment. I revealed to her that my white walls were getting stale and that I needed some colored pictures to hang up. Shocked, first that I would know she enjoyed drawing, and second that I asked her for a picture, Zora excitedly agreed to make me some portraits. As she drew, I asked her about the colors she intended to use and why. Becoming increasingly engaged by my questions, she gave me an elaborate explanation of what these certain colors meant to her. Blue because it reminds her of a cool sea. Red simply because it's fun. Orange signifies the beauty of fire. Every day for two weeks I had a new picture to talk about with her. From a girl who typically ignored me, this was a major breakthrough! We were building a real-life connection that was no longer so intimidating to her.

As the months passed, the momentum kept growing. I started off one day by telling her how cool her hair looked. I recited all of the different styles I had seen her with and asked how they were the same or different. I was truly fascinated by the mix of braids, coils, twists, puffs, zigs, and zags. I asked her about what techniques were used and what products worked best to keep them all together. Soon after, I began to hear all about her foster sister and how nice she was to Zora, the elements of her "style," and how Zora had fun feeling like a grown woman having her hair done every morning.

As time went on, my relationship with Zora continued to deepen. Not only did she begin to open up to me about very personal and emotionally evocative pieces of her life, she was much more cooperative and helpful throughout the groups I conducted. The little girl who normally didn't participate was now helping me as my assistant. She began to thrive in the program, and I like to think that our strong bond had something to do with it. Through my experience with her, I learned that my success (and ultimate happiness!) in this work was built on the sincere and genuine relationships I built with these children. The imprint of this experience served as a constant reminder about how I could reach other kids like her. And I'm proud to say I did.

Looking back, I can see that I benefitted from my relationship with Zora and the other children I got to know as well. Perhaps I learned more from them than they did from me. I eventually learned that developing relationships wasn't really that difficult after all. My efforts and experience with Zora showed me how simple, yet powerful, relationships can be. Just by taking one small moment to show I knew something about Zora's uniqueness, the door was opened just enough that I could begin to captivate her attention and, more significantly, her trust.

Brent Bolstrom is a research assistant at Search Institute in Minneapolis, Minnesota. He's particularly interested in studying resiliency indicators in children and how protective factors can buffer them against adversity and stress. Brent enjoys reading, running marathons, and watching his two nieces grow.

An Old-Fashioned Apprenticeship

～

History is full of stories of famous partnerships—the mentor sharing the full range of her or his experience with a young person who eventually comes into her or his own. Sometimes the young person deliberately seeks out the mentor; sometimes the mentor just appears. The impact of these relationships—even if they're short—unfolds over time, and the true worth of what's exchanged may not be perceived until much later. In many cases, it's not just the young person who is positively affected, but the mentor as well. The stories in this section tell of alert adults who saw opportunities in their work to support young people in developing their interests and who often learned something about themselves along the way.

JONATHAN LETHEM

A Very Present and
Interesting Friend

The first day Jonathan Lethem walked into Michael Seidenberg's used bookstore, the two struck up a conversation that has lasted 26 years.

The 14-year-old Jonathan had a hunger for books, fueled in part by his own inclinations and further fed by his mother's voracious reading habits and her enthusiasm for both writers and books. He had thought he knew every inch of the few funny, diverse, scruffy blocks of the Boerum Hill neighborhood of Brooklyn that he called home, but he'd never seen this bookstore called The Brazen Head before. And what in the world did "Brazen Head" mean, anyway? Of course he had to go in.

Michael, the owner, had trained as an actor in college, so he exuded an appealing sense of theatricality. His partner was a puppeteer, and the modular bookshelves were easily moved to create a performance space. To Jonathan, 24-year-old Michael had a great adult presence, enhanced by the big black beard he wore.

"Michael combined a great sense of humor and a great sense

of performance," recalls Jonathan. "He was very charismatic and funny. His slightly grouchy authority made it seem as though he'd been there a million years, but I knew he hadn't. I enjoyed his ability to tease everyone, yet express an enormous amount of affection, which implied you were worthy of being the object of a joke. I think you could say he became my first 'grown-up' friend."

In 1978, Jonathan had already been exposed to the rather bohemian adult world of his parents. His father was a painter, and his mother was a social worker and neighborhood organizer. Their eclectic interests and liberal politics produced a semi-communal environment through which flowed "very present and very interesting" friends. Jonathan was the oldest of three children who liked making friends with adults, reveling in the strength and diversity of his parents' self-made community. His mother's death from a brain tumor around this time caused some of that strength at home to unravel, and Jonathan found himself naturally drawn to other adults for friendship and support.

Michael was a unique teacher, enticing Jonathan into a rather old-fashioned sort of apprenticeship that centered on books. He patiently initiated the teenager into the mysteries of understanding what mattered about a used book's condition. "Michael drew me into the bookstore by imparting his own sense of the value of overlooked things," says Jonathan. "First editions by obscure authors were much, much more precious than first editions by those authors everyone knew and read, and so my own instinct for the valuable secrets of modern literature was confirmed by Michael's. And the smallness of the bookstore, the implicit, beautiful futility of dedicating your life to what you loved, no matter how little reward it would bring, was always one of his greatest lessons."

Michael's suggestions about new authors to read expanded Jonathan's literary universe, and the fact that he was a book collector confirmed Jonathan's own tendency to be an accumulator. As Jonathan started hanging out at the bookstore, Michael also put him to work shelving books, cleaning, and working behind the counter.

The subtext to their relationship was the death of Jonathan's mother. "He must have known," says Jonathan, looking back, "but it was terrifically important for me in the way I organized my own identity to survive and thrive that I needed to tell people I was fine and have them consent to that. He could probably see behind that, but very generously took my word for it."

At a critical time in both Jonathan's emotional and professional development, Michael helped him confirm his own budding sense about books—that personal taste was enormously important and that no matter how many famous or contemporary writers there might be, an *author* would have a secret shelf of favorites. Taking the last gift his mother gave him before she died—a manual typewriter—Jonathan, at 15, taught himself to type and wrote his first novel.

"Michael was hardly a typical kind of mentor," says Jonathan. "He was kind of a rascal, a bon vivant, who lived a very free and easy life. He influenced my life as a reader and guided me toward my career in writing enormously in the kinds of things he read and steered me towards. He also took me seriously, but not with any reverence. He'd frown or groan or make a joke if I did or said something that didn't impress him."

With the visibility his own work has brought him, Jonathan now finds himself able to bring readers to obscure writers he loves by championing reprints and writing their introductions. He's also able to expand the worldview of writing students in his work as a teacher at summer programs at various universities around the country and the Clarion Writers Workshop in East Lansing, Michigan.

"I'm pressing books into others' hands, reminding them of the importance of new writing. I want my students to read not just what's fashionable. I do try to extend Michael's passionate lessons from his bookstore into the classroom when I teach now or in individual encounters with students. I want them to write what they love and not be embarrassed or obey anyone else's idea of what's important. Once you find what you love, be fierce about it. That sensibility really comes from Michael. By sharing his full range of experience and response to me, Michael helped me know myself."

— *Jonathan Lethem has published six novels as well as short stories, essays, and introductions, writing from Brooklyn, not far from where he grew up on Dean Street. His most recent book is* Fortress of Solitude, *and he won the 1999 National Book Critics Circle Award for* Motherless Brooklyn. *Jonathan's father, Richard, is 71 and still painting. The name of Michael Seidenberg's bookstore, The Brazen Head, comes from the title of a book by John Cowper Powys. Michael is still selling books online, and Jonathan sees him often.*

Eva Vanessa Barragan and
Sonya Clark-Herrera

Designing Relationships, Making Art

~

Sonya Clark-Herrera's passion and career as an art historian and educator had taken her from graduate school at Columbia University in New York City to a stint as an artist's representative. When she resettled in East Palo Alto, California, she found herself brainstorming with her longtime artist partner, Omar Ramirez, and her husband, Eugene Clark-Herrera, a teacher-turned-lawyer, about what to do for young people who had nothing better to do than "tag" local businesses with graffiti. They decided to try something familiar to them—building relationships through art.

"I love working with teenagers. I *need* to work with teenagers," she says. "And I love using art as the lens to discuss their situation."

By "their situation," Sonya means the economic and social disadvantages faced by young people aged 14 to 18 in the East Palo Alto community where she lives. The increasingly accelerated growth in this Bay Area city has displaced many local residents, disconnecting young people from friends and a newly revitalized downtown they hardly recognize.

"We'd done public art for communities many times across the country," says Sonya of her long-term relationship with muralist Ramirez. "Why couldn't kids do it?" What the three friends thought would be simply a summer project begun in 2001 has now evolved into a very successful, full-time program called the East Palo Alto Mural Art Project. The core of the project's work is to provide opportunities for young people to produce public art. A key component is that young people delve deep into local history before painting murals in various neighborhoods. What blossoms as a result of the work is a complex new web of relationships among adults and youth that goes well beyond a single project.

Eva Vanessa Barragan is one member of a team of 20–25 teens employed by the art project to assist with the research, design, fabrication, installation, and unveiling of a mural. "Sonya has really opened up my world," says Vanessa, a junior at Sacred Heart Prep School. "Every month she's handing me something new to do."

Youth apply to attend a project-sponsored training seminar and are interviewed by a hiring panel before undergoing a formal ten-week program during which they are paid between $9.00 and $15.00 an hour for their work, depending on their roles. Presented with the theme for each mural, the teens spend five weeks working with a muralist, conducting extensive historical research, and creating a mural design. The teens then work for the next five weeks fabricating and installing their mural. Each mural program closes with an unveiling and community celebration to recognize the teens and to provide them with a forum for presenting their mural to the community. The Mural Project is currently producing a series of 12 large public pieces of art for each school in the Ravenswood School District.

Vanessa met Sonya at the Boys and Girls Club. Sonya invited Vanessa to apply for a job with the project when she discovered the teen's interest in painting. The two have developed a close friendship as a result of working together. "Sonya is like my boss in a way," says Vanessa, "but she's also my friend. She's busy, but she always has time to teach me. She invites me to go along to meetings of her board of directors to see what that's like, but she also makes me part of her life. She makes me feel as if I have an important role because she asks me what I want to do."

The murals range in size from a 10' x 5' project created to commemorate community day at Stanford University to an 80' x 11' diptych honoring farm workers at the Cesar Chavez Academy. It's not just their size that makes the murals stand out, but the eye-popping color and symbolic complexity of each one. Fists rise up from the ground in one mural, for example, representing the predominant East Palo Alto cultural communities of Pacific Islander, Latino, and African-American through cultural iconography tattooed to the wrists. In another, enormous white lilies symbolize the beauty of the community while a confident African American young man symbolizes the area's youth.

It's during the historical research that local community leaders are invited to speak to the young artists, and here is where Sonya says an unexpected, additional benefit has developed. "As it turns out, the adults who've come to lecture the young people are telling us that they feel more connected, too. It's good for adults to feel respected by teens just as much as it's good for teens to be respected by adults."

Many of the youth involved in the project realize a wide range of benefits from participating, in addition to the opportunity to develop their artistic and social skills. The project constantly brings them into contact with a variety of positive adults, allows teens to mentor younger children, and increases their status in their community because their work also allows some to contribute financially to their families. "Some of our young people make more per hour than their parents," says Sonya. "It's a drop in the bucket in their overall financial situation, but it means a lot to the family. It contributes to building respect for the youth and helps their relationships with their parents flourish."

Besides feeling that her family is proud of the work she's doing, Vanessa says she's been invited to participate in other adult-youth partnerships, become more active in her community about environmental issues, and even sold some of her own work at local galleries. "I've been involved in community service in my own little world, but I'm getting to do things countywide. I get to see more. I had never really felt respected by adults, but now I do. It feels great that they ask us questions and want to know about us."

"Most of the people I know are jealous of the life I have working with these crazy kids," says Sonya. "I listen to them, and I remember what I felt like at that age. I work very closely with our staff to help them remember when they were 14 so we all learn how to do this work without shoving it down anybody's throat. The teens have a huge impact on the people they work with, and I'm lucky enough to do work that I think is making a difference in their lives, too."

— *The families of Eva Vanessa Barragan and Sonya and Eugene Clark-Herrera like to spend time together in the summer. In addition to having young people over and taking some on camping trips, Sonya and Eugene are parents of three-year-old son Eldridge and one-year-old Michaela. Sonya says her son in particular adores Vanessa.*

Becky Judd

Get Those Butterflies Raging

~

It was going to be a long, lousy, boring vacation for 17-year-old Becky Judd. After a speeding ticket and three car accidents, 1970 wasn't turning out to be such a great year. It didn't matter to the rebellious teenager that it was her own fault for getting in trouble and losing the privilege of going to Mexico with her family. She only knew she was going to be stuck at home in rainy Portland, Oregon, and miss her family's spring break in a warm, tropical place.

Enter "Rabbit."

Rabbit had been a family friend ever since Becky could remember. A librarian by training, working at the Portland Art Museum, he had befriended Becky's mother, a museum volunteer. Rabbit was one of a cadre of interesting, artistic adult friends that Becky considered "cool." He never married or had his own kids but instead became close to several families with whom he spent so much time, and he became like family. He was a mountaineer, a Mazama, Oregon, mountain guide who frequently led people on trips around the Northwest and into the Himalayan Mountains. He liked to foster relationships between the outdoors and his "chosen family" members. He had a particular affinity for the river, and he decided it was time to introduce Becky to the river, too.

Rabbit invited Becky (and the adult "chaperone" her parents had left in charge) to join him and some other friends for a three-day wilderness river trip down the Deschutes River that runs through north central Oregon. Unbeknownst to Becky, Rabbit had negotiated this idea with her mother before she left, knowing Becky was going to be stuck at home. "I didn't have anything else to do, so I said yes," says Becky. "I think he felt sorry for me."

Rabbit warned Becky that while she'd be with the group, she'd have to float down the river in her own boat because there wasn't enough room for her in the Mackenzie-style riverboats the others would be using. Becky had floated around in boats and inner tubes before, so she thought it wouldn't be a problem. But when she arrived with Rabbit at the river, she discovered that her boat was actually a small, yellow life raft that looked like something salvaged from a fishing boat of another era! There wasn't even a place for her to actually sit down in it, so Rabbit helped her scavenge some scrap wood from a nearby abandoned cabin to fashion a raft-like frame that provided a little more structure and a seat to sit on.

Rabbit had brought oars, but then discovered that Becky didn't know how to use them, so she got a crash course on paddling in white water. The group put into the river at Bend, Oregon, with the intention of floating some 60 miles down the Deschutes into the Columbia River. The next thing Becky knew, she was headed for the rush of rapids.

"Rabbit really changed my life with that trip. He had total confidence in me that I could row down this big, charging river. It was the perfect place to use my adolescent adrenaline. I could have a place for a thrill, surrounded by other people, but I could also go to the river to center myself and cool out."

Along the way, the group stopped at night to camp out in the open in high desert. "I'd only slept out in the yard or gone to kid's camp," says Becky. "I'd never slept out in the wilderness under clear, starry nights with the smell of sagebrush and the crackling of a fire." Wherever the group camped, Rabbit would spin stories, embellishing found tales and folklore of the Northwest. "One of my favorites was about the Stumbo brothers who closed Interstate 5 one New Year's Eve back in the 1950s because they thought they owned part of the freeway. You couldn't leave because his stories would just unravel for hours."

Becky's teenage turmoil of rebellion and her craving for excitement began to quiet during her three days on the river. She had always been headstrong, athletic, and independent, but the thrill and feeling of accomplishment from navigating her own boat through the crashing waves and whitewater helped her begin to focus. The rhythm of the river and the steady, quiet comfort of the desert gave her time to reflect on her life and what she really wanted out of it.

Becky discovered what would become a lifelong passion and has since taken many river and wilderness trips, some with the now 80 year old Rabbit. Her love blossomed into kayaking, leading her to win a spot on the U.S. kayaking team and a gold medal in the World Championships for white-water slalom kayaking in 1979. She still finds herself applying the lessons she learned from Rabbit in working with youth as the Alaska Division of Behavioral Health's Resiliency and Youth Development Specialist.

"Rather than judging me by my mistakes, Rabbit seemed to see some goodness and potential in me, and by inviting me on that river trip, he opened up doors of possibilities for me. Now when I work with teens, I realize that in the natural course of development, they're bound to make mistakes. It's important for us as adults to help them learn from those mistakes by providing them with challenging opportunities to learn new talents, a sense of self, and confidence. I tell young people to get out of their comfort zone, find something that scares them, and work with that. Get those butterflies raging. Feel the fear of taking healthy risks, do it anyway, and revel in the accomplishment of trying and sometimes succeeding."

While Becky has held many types of jobs throughout her career, what she's become is a teacher. She tries to reflect the kind of coaching Rabbit provided for her. She uses it to help young people see that the challenges they overcome in one area of their lives can carry over into other areas. "As a teacher I found that if I can help my students overcome the fear of rafting on white water or giving a speech in front of a group, it gives them the confidence to tackle other difficult issues in their lives."

— *Becky Judd relocated to Alaska 20 years ago when she was recruited to teach Inupiaq Eskimos how to kayak. As part of her work for the state, she and her best friend, Derek Peterson, helped launch a statewide initiative to bring the Developmental Assets framework to Alaskan communities. She also helped establish the Spirit of Youth organization, which creates and promotes opportunities for youth engagement across Alaska.*

Becoming That Hero

By the time he was sent to work for Chuck Wolf, 14-year-old Dameon Willich had already been trained by some of the best horsemen in the country. Dameon had been riding horses since he was four, when he was first put atop a little paint by his mother. He hated horses at first, but his mother loved them, and since his older brother was allergic, he was the one chosen to ride. She hoped Chuck could teach her unruly teenager something about hard work and the horse industry.

Chuck Wolf ran Bridle Trails Stables in Kirkland, Washington, and subjected Dameon to an old-fashioned, almost medieval-style apprenticeship. The boy lived with Wolf's family during the spring and summer months, working alongside Chuck's own kids from sunup to sundown, just like everyone else in the horse business. Chuck's business was to buy unbroken, green horses down in Oregon and bring them back to be trained and sold. The faster the better in order to turn a profit.

"I look back now and realize the things I learned working for that man," says Dameon. "I had been trained by some of the best professional horsemen in the world, but Chuck was more like an old-time cowboy horseman. You learned things from him that you wouldn't learn in the showring, like how to break, train, and turn out a horse in 90 days. He would make me do menial tasks over and over again so that repetition became instinctual. I was a lot like some of those headstrong horses in those days and too rebellious at the time to appreciate the lessons I was learning, but he really taught me a lot about life and the way you needed to take pride in the work you do."

Dameon performed, competed, and won awards on horseback. When he wasn't living with Chuck's family, he was at home, going to school, and trying to follow in his older brother's footsteps academically. The two often fought, their personalities clashing, and Dameon didn't get along with his stepfather at home, either. He started holding back money from his winnings and giving it to a friend for safekeeping until he could afford to have the friend buy him a motorcycle. At age 15½, Dameon left home to strike out on his own.

During his time on the road, he fell in with a group of bikers, who, like Chuck, took an interest in helping him. "They kept my nose to the grindstone to a certain degree. Whenever we'd stop long enough in one place, they always made sure I went back to school." Dameon ended up going to eight different high schools before settling back down in rural Washington, and starting college.

Still restless and living alone in his early 20s, Dameon decided to move back to Seattle in 1976. He went back to doing what he knew best—caring for horses. Another old horseman named Jack Riley stepped in, when no one else would, to give this wild kid a job at the Aqua Barn Ranch in Maple Valley. "He told me years later he thought I would become an asset to the ranch," recalls Dameon, "but at the time I was still a 'hard ride,' the term we used for horses that were going to be really hard to break. I was a disillusioned young man with little idea where I was going, which is why I fell back on horses." Working on commission seven days a week year-round, Dameon went from mucking out stalls to training young riders as the barn's day camp coordinator, then teaching western riding as well.

In 1978 a group called Sagittarius Productions came to Jack with a proposal. They wanted to start a new enterprise in the Puget Sound—a Renaissance Faire—and they wanted Jack as a partner. What they also got was Dameon, who by now was running Jack's stables, as their liaison to the ranch. "Some of the members of the group had done a lot of stunt work and [it] included two former Olympic fencers, but the next thing you know, I'm telling them what to do with the horses, and after that, I just fell in with them." The group's fledgling efforts eventually failed, but now Dameon was hooked on the whole idea of researching history, riding horses, and using weapons at the same time.

After a few false starts, Dameon finally refined his idea of performing with weapons and horse by basing the work on stagecraft instead of martial arts, making the use of weaponry safer. He founded the Seattle Knights in 1992. Working at a friend's ranch with a core group of seven horses that came to be known as the "Magnificent Seven," he launched his performing company and a school to train actors and stunt artists, based on his own performance fight system.

Today more than 400 people have gone through the Seattle Knights academy, and the company regularly performs at fairs and festivals on the West Coast. Many members of the company—and their horses—also perform as stunt actors in films such as Kevin Costner's *The Postman*. The academy's shows are written to not only be fun, but also subtly teach children and adults, with a strong subtext of equality, about a code of honor.

Women fight on equal footing with men, and the good guys (in many cases, the women or the shorter guy) always win.

Dameon and his wife, Darragh Metzger, a fantasy writer and accomplished horsewoman with the Knights, have no children of their own, but Dameon says he always felt it was his destiny to participate in raising other people's kids. "I learned as I was growing up how to hurt people, but now I teach children and adults how *not* to hurt people. I live my life playing, and I try to show children—and adults, for that matter—that they can play. You don't have to grow up and just be old, you just have to be responsible."

The lessons that Dameon learned from Chuck Wolf and Jack Riley still resonate with him, long after these two old horseman have passed on: the value of training and discipline, the pride in your work, and, eventually, the value of trying to make your own dreams come true and help others realize their dreams as well. "You can see by the way little kids look at you when you perform that they idolize you," says Dameon. "You have just made something come true that they have only seen on TV or read about in books. You've become their hero, and you have a responsibility to be that hero."

— *Dameon Willich and Darragh Metzger are actors, artists, and authors living in western Washington with their horses, Shanarra, Terra Cotta, and Rafael Luz de Dios. Despite the fact that they work in three of the hardest professions in which to make a living, they love it and continue to share the wonder of their world with others through their art.*

Roberta Greenwood tells
how a tough teacher
brought out the best in her.

ROBERTA GREENWOOD

You Can Do This

❦

"You're not going to waste your talents in *my* classroom; now . . . go write."

With that, the tall, imposing woman quietly closed the door to the teacher's lounge and left me, a shy, unpopular 8th grader, with my first assignment: write 10 additional parts for the 9th-grade play. Pacing in the forbidden sanctuary, I wondered what I could've possibly done to deserve such a punishment; it was 1966 and no student at Hilltop Junior High School in Chula Vista, California, willingly entered the teacher's lounge. I couldn't believe the bad luck that had come my way—and I wouldn't understand until decades had passed how meaningful her words to me would prove to be.

My teacher, Mary-Lynn Deddeh, had earned the moniker "Dead-eye" early in her career. Some thought it was a simple mispronunciation of her Iraqi surname, but those in the know recognized it as a tribute to her uncanny ability to spot irrepressible junior high school boys bent on ditching school. Five years earlier, my older brother Roger had suffered greatly in her honors English class, and I was terrified by the prospect of spending a semester with her in our mandatory drama workshop. She was the only teacher I had ever met who unfailingly made eye contact with her students and on occasion would tell me to get my hair out of my eyes. "I want to see your soul in action," she would say. How did she know, I wondered, that my hair formed a wall to keep the sneers of my peers out and hide my tears?

That day, I faced an empty pad of paper and questioned how I would ever write 10 speaking parts for a western comedy titled *They Went That-Away.* I didn't even like the play and, as an 8th grader, wouldn't be allowed to try out for a speaking role. Why did she pick me out of a classroom of 30 students anyway? I sat, deep in my misery, and sulked. Up until that day, my writing had been limited to required essays and other written assignments; oh, except for that note she'd intercepted the other day in class. That was it! She was punishing me. My brother was right; she was a tyrant.

As the 45-minute punishment came to an end, she poked her head into the dark lounge and asked how it was going. My silent response only brought a laugh; "Well, you'll just do it again to-morrow. See you then."

And so it went for several weeks; each day, Mrs. Deddeh would send me to the teacher's lounge with the same command: "Write." Each day, she would check on my progress and send me scurrying to my earth science class with her admonition: "You have greatness in you. You can do this." In spite of myself, I began to wonder if she could be right.

One French maid, two wayward cowboys, a few churlish ranchers, and even a runaway Indian later, I had completed my task. I was as amazed as anyone. Each day, she coaxed me into the imaginary world that all writers inhabit—she urged me to let go and have fun, invent myself on the page and stretch my imagina-tion. Along the way she taught me a bit about plot development, dialogue and dialects, the importance of a walk-on part, how to whistle louder than any living person, and, most importantly, that I was a writer who had ideas that mattered. She listened to me, granted me the freedom to explore ideas in new ways, and she believed in me.

At the last performance of the play, she called me on stage and presented me with the Drama Student of the Year award and a warm embrace. A few weeks earlier, I would've cringed at her touch—that evening, I felt surrounded by her light and wisdom. With my hair pulled back into a tight ponytail, I looked into the eyes of my first audience and basked in the glow. That hug has stretched through more than 30 years, four children, three marriages, countless rejections, and several publications. She became and remains my best friend.

When my premier essay appeared in a national publication, she received the first copy. Her words to me were "Great work—I always knew you could do it. Now, how about helping out at a performance camp for teens next week?"

— *Roberta Greenwood is a freelance writer living in Bellevue, Washington. She and "Dead-Eye" still enjoy theater together, as well as all things chocolate, their collective gang of four grandchildren, and evenings spent with The Old Broads, a feisty group of amazing women in San Diego, California.*

Simple Gifts

The lyrics of an old Shaker hymn tell of the freedom of simple gifts that allow us to "come down where we ought to be." Growing up is about exploring options, figuring out who we are and how to make the best of ourselves. But sometimes life interferes with the business of life. Events cause us to lose confidence, then hope. Choices and even loved ones are taken from us. But the stories in this section tell of adults who seized a moment in a young person's life. They noticed, they listened, they spoke, they acted. Lives were changed for the better, and these young people received simple gifts that allowed them to grow up and reach out to other children.

Unexpected Turns

At an evening workshop Keith Pattinson conducted several years ago about strengthening the relationships between adults and youth in the community, he noticed a middle-aged woman break into tears and leave the room. She later participated in the balance of the event and was one of several folks who lined up to talk with him personally at the conclusion. This is the story she told him.

When Maria was a 13-year-old in 7th grade, she lived with her mom and dad and had earned honour roll status in her Canadian junior high school. Things were great at school but a challenge at home with her dad's addiction to alcohol, a hardship made bearable by the consistent love, encouragement, and support she received from her mom. Eventually, however, the mother's battle to deal with the father's drinking led to her own addiction to prescription drugs, and Maria's life took a turn for the worse in 8th grade.

"The only subject I was passing was English," this woman told Keith. "In February of that year, our English teacher gave us an assignment to write a story or poem about ourselves. I thought long and hard about it and decided maybe if I told people what was going on in my life, someone would listen and maybe tell me what I should do. I spent hours on that poem because it gave me a chance to share something important to me and gave me hope someone would listen."

However, the young woman was devastated when her corrected work was returned to her a week later covered in red ink and a failing mark. An accelerated decline in her attitude and behavior at home and school culminated one day months later when she was summoned over the school's public address system to the principal's office.

"This is all I need on top of everything else that's going on in my life," this young woman thought as she shuffled down the hall. "Now I'm going to get kicked out of school."

In the principal's office, she candidly asked him why she was there.

"It's about your poem, Maria."

Assuming the worst, she told him she was sorry.

"Actually, it's my turn to apologize to you," the principal said. He went on to explain that while doing a review of classroom work a few months before, he'd come across her poem and thought it was one of the most powerful, moving poems he'd ever read. Without her permission, he had submitted the poem to a province-wide writing competition. He said it had been wrong for him to do so secretly, but he was concerned that the last thing she needed was another disappointment if the poem didn't receive some recognition.

The principal handed her a book published as a result of that writing competition, explaining that her poem had been given the highest recognition in the entire province.

He told her he now understood better what was happening in her life and wanted her to have the book as a reminder that she could achieve any goals she set for herself. He and all her teachers wanted her to know that from now on, they'd help any way they could.

Maria bounced down the hall saying to herself, "I can be anything I want!" Within a year, she was back on the honour roll and graduated from high school and university with honours—all because one man took five minutes to tell her that he understood, that she was okay, and that he and others would be there for her.

—

After telling Keith her story, Maria explained that she had burst into tears that evening because she realized, for the first time in 40 years, that she couldn't remember the name of the man who had changed her life in a matter of minutes.

— Keith Pattinson is a father and grandfather who travels throughout Canada telling the Developmental Assets story. He has spoken to hundreds of audiences and has been acknowledged as a Master Storyteller and one of his country's most inspiring, motivating presenters. Asset building is the foundation of the keynotes and workshops he offers to children, teens, families, and communities.

MARIANNE PIEPER

The Smallest Gesture

By age 16, Marianne Pieper of Golden Valley, Minnesota, had already experienced a lifetime of tragedies. She had lost her father, who died when she was just a year and a half old. When Marianne was 13, her mother, Virginia Webster, found out she had breast cancer the same day her grandmother was killed in a car accident. And her stepfather was beginning to unravel under the pressures of family life.

The family struggled with Virginia's illness for several years until, in 1972, a pregnancy forced Virginia to consider an abortion. Her doctors urged this option because they felt they could not give chemotherapy to a pregnant woman, but Virginia couldn't bear the thought of losing the baby, so she refused treatment. Virginia gave birth to a healthy baby, but 18 months later succumbed to cancer.

Before she died, Virginia had arranged with administrators at Robbinsdale High School for Marianne to start classes an hour late so she could help her younger siblings get ready for school. Virginia had also decided that it would be best for close family friends to assume legal guardianship of Marianne's youngest brother, Preston, and Marianne says the day Preston left was one of the hardest things she ever faced.

"Preston was only 1½," says Marianne. "He used to call me 'Mom.' I think he was quite a confused little kid. On a winter day in 1974, we took Preston to our friend's house and left him there. He had a terrible cold, and he cried. My mom was home in bed. It was a heartbreaking day for me. I can't imagine what it was like for her."

Virginia died four months later. Marianne's stepfather, whose drinking had worsened as his wife's health declined, fell apart after Virginia's death and was eventually diagnosed with bipolar disorder. Marianne, the oldest daughter at home, stepped up to assume responsibility for raising her younger siblings.

Marianne tried to emulate the grace and dignity with which her mother had met such extraordinary challenges. "I became the main cook and caretaker because I wanted to. I read to my brothers and sisters because my mother read to me. I sang to them at bedtime because she sang to me. She guided us with love and kindness."

Not surprisingly, despite the help and support of family, friends, church, and neighbors, Marianne had been having a difficult time emotionally through her mother's illness. Her science teacher, Harvey Hummel, noticed. "He was a terrific teacher," says Marianne, "a short, dark-haired, middle-aged man who loved science and wanted us to love it, too. He always gestured with wild enthusiasm as he taught."

Harvey Hummel found ways to let Marianne know she mattered to him. He always asked why she'd missed school if she was absent. She was often one of the last people to class, and he would always say something encouraging and funny to her. He made a tape of a song called "Down by the Seaside, Maryann," and welcomed her to class by starting the tape and singing along while doing the cha-cha.

The piano had been a part of Marianne's life, too. She had taken lessons for eight years, but as a sophomore, with her mother close to death, it became clear to her that she was going to have to give it up. There were too many responsibilities at home and in school to keep taking lessons. She casually mentioned to Harvey at school that she would be giving her last piano recital that night. That was all she said.

"Somehow he found out who my piano teacher was and came to the recital," recalls Marianne. "I didn't know he was there until I stood up to announce my number and saw him sitting there, smiling at me. Usually someone from my family would always come, but this happened at a time when my mom was very ill.

"It was such a little thing, but it sent a very powerful message to me. He had made an effort to get there, which is not something that any other teacher I knew would do. It gave me hope that there would continue to be people in my life who would 'show up' when I needed them. It really buoyed me up."

Despite the many struggles and losses she faced as a young woman, Marianne went on to have a life full of love, family, friends, challenging work, and deep involvement in her church. She has five children ages 13 to 21 to whom she's tried to give the kind of love and support her mother gave to her. In her work as Ohio School Board chair and the asset mobilizer for the Together We Care initiative in Hartford, Kentucky, she supports youth and teaches community members how to do the same. She is particularly fond of telling teachers the story of her life and Harvey Hummel's kindness. "I don't think they always understand how much power they have to change the lives of children with just a few words, just a few hours of their time."

Marianne works in the same building as her district's high school Alternative Learning Program (ALP). Twice a day staff march students to their meals in the cafeteria. Students must hold their arms behind their backs and are not allowed to speak. Marianne always says good morning anyway. While at an academic event with her son at a middle school in a neighboring county, a young man she didn't recognize suddenly said, "You're the lady that says hello to us every day at the ALP!" They got acquainted, and now Marianne calls him by name every day when he passes.

"Nurturing young people has been the focus of my adult life," says Marianne. "I love to smile and speak to them. I like to remember that all young people—especially the struggling ones—have a story. We just need to listen and understand."

— *Marianne still has contact with her youngest brother, Preston, plays the piano at church, and teaches little kids. She credits her husband with being a patient, kind man who also happens to be a laundry expert. Her family likes to play tennis at midnight and have "Wild Thing" suppers—a tradition of which she cannot divulge the details.*

JULIANNE JAZ

Don't Buckle Under

The small, 69-bed hospital in Carson City, Nevada, had become like home since Julianne Jaz started working there as a candy striper three years before in 1968. Smart and eager to learn, she had become the hospital's youngest employee when she was hired at 15 and had trained in almost every patient-oriented division. Everyone on the staff liked her, and several of the doctors had taken her under their wings after she expressed an interest in someday going to medical school.

One evening, although Julianne usually worked in the emergency room (ER), she had been assigned to work "float" on the surgical floors. Partway through her shift, she was surprised to see a fellow high school student named Doug arrive on the floor; he had come up to give Julianne some bad news: her ex-fiancé's brother was down in the ER with a gunshot wound in his gut.

Seventeen-year-old Julianne made her way quickly through the halls of the hospital on her way to the emergency room. "I went down to the emergency room out of respect for the family," recalls Julianne, "not knowing what I was about to walk into." Doug, in a misguided attempt to be helpful, had given Julianne the wrong information. The gunshot victim in the ER was actually Julianne's ex-fiancé, Richard, not his brother, and the wound had been self-inflicted.

Julianne was supported by her hospital "family" members, who closed ranks around her and tried to help her through the shock. Richard's attempted suicide was the culminating event in a series of upheavals Julianne had been subjected to during the latter part of high school involving Richard's family as well as her own. What Julianne would not know for several more years was that she and her younger sister were purchased from a black-market adoption ring operating out of 1950s Las Vegas and that her father's car repair business was actually a mob front. The impact of these events were leading her parents into personal and financial ruin; Julianne only knew that her parents were pressuring her to put a good face on the family by doing well in school and getting married as soon as possible.

"I had this supportive milieu at the hospital," says Julianne, "while in another part of my life was my alcoholic father and my mentally ill mother. My parents' problems were related to all these things they knew about but kept hidden from my sister and me. My mother was in a lot of emotional pain about not being able to have children of her own. My father forced these adoptions on her to add to the front he created to appear normal to the outside world. As I got older, she wanted to clamp down on me, and one way was to insist that I find one person to date in high school and then get married."

Richard had been the first boy in high school who showed any attention to Julianne, and her mother decided that, because he looked as though he came from a good family, he was the one. At first he seemed funny and smart and when he started to talk about marriage, Julianne went along because she was lonely and hungry for attention. She and Richard started having sex, which further complicated their relationship. Spending time with Richard's family, Julianne began to witness the alcoholism and violence in his parents' marriage and it frightened her. As the relationship continued, Richard became increasingly possessive. Julianne started to feel trapped.

As she approached graduation, Julianne also began to discover areas of success for herself that put the dysfunction in her family and relationship with Richard in sharper relief. She continued working 30 hours a week at the hospital, making straight A's in school, and was designated valedictorian of her senior class. Her personal physician, Dr. James Fulper, worked at the hospital and, along with cardiologist Dr. Ben Harper, had been mentoring Julianne, even beginning to suggest ways she could finance medical school as she approached graduation. She also met another boy who seemed to be everything Richard wasn't and fell in love with him. The emotional pressure on Julianne continued to build as she and Richard began to move through their senior year. The supportive network of adults at the hospital could see that Julianne was struggling, but many people felt that they should stay out of someone else's family issues. Unable to see an escape from her family situation at this point, Julianne became increasingly depressed.

Partway through their senior year, Julianne accidentally discovered that Richard was making down payments on an engagement ring. She feared that a marriage to Richard would inevitably mirror his parent's destructive marriage. "I was having sex to get affection, but had fooled myself into thinking it was okay because we were going to get married eventually," says Julianne. "Finding out about the ring led me to one of the few pieces of insight I had at that age. I believed one of us wouldn't survive. So I broke up with Richard."

Richard embarked upon an escalating series of strategies

aimed at forcing Julianne to marry him. First, he announced he would become a priest, which didn't sway her. Then he revealed to Julianne's parents that they had been having sex, which cemented the parents' conviction that the two young people should marry. The pressure from her parents to renew the engagement ramped up. When it became clear that Julianne wouldn't change her mind, Richard appeared at her house one morning before she went to work to announce dramatically that anything that happened from then on was *her* fault.

That was the night that he shot himself with a .357.

Richard did not die, but spent six weeks in the hospital telling everyone he could collar that it was Julianne's fault that he had shot himself—all while Julianne continued working 30 hours a week in the hospital and going to school. Both sets of parents now banded together, at one point even sitting Julianne down in the living room while all four adults dictated to the young girl the course her life was going to take, including marrying Richard. The four adults also forced her to go to her senior prom with Richard when he got out of the hospital. "My mother bought my corsage and Richard appeared to drive me to the prom. I didn't have much opportunity to take a stand." Being forced further and further into a situation she did not want brought Julianne close to contemplating suicide.

One day just after the prom, Dr. Harper and Dr. Fulper sought out Julianne on her shift and took her aside in one of the facility's exam rooms. "I remember them saying that they knew I was a straight-arrow kid," Julianne says of that day, "that I had done everything I possibly could to obey my parents and do well in school. But they also said, 'Don't buckle under. We're telling you that what your parents are telling you to do is wrong. You have to do something else.'"

It was as if someone took the young woman by the shoulders

and just pointed her off at a 45-degree angle. "I felt that for the first time in my life, someone had seen what was really happening and that they understood the impact it was having on me. Their act engendered in me a discovery of my own will and survivorship that just couldn't be denied. I realized I wouldn't kill myself, and I was going to get out of there. They took to heart their responsibility as adults in this situation. I crossed a threshold."

Emboldened by this support and on the verge of graduation and her 18th birthday, Julianne decided to take action—she left home within days of finishing high school. "What those two doctors said was such a revelation to me at that age," says Julianne. "Their act helped me see that I didn't have to fall in line."

While Julianne still faced many challenges later in life, she did escape what could have been a disastrous marriage and was set upon a path in which she was not only able to break free of the negative influences of her family, but go on to help others. She eventually founded and ran the first domestic violence program in Craig, Colorado, in 1978 when she was only 25. Later, while in college, she did a course of independent study and examined why a sexual assault crisis line at her university campus had failed some years before. Her research led her to reestablish an improved crisis line.

Today, Julianne is especially conscious of trying to give back to children the gift of courage she received. "I have really endeavored wherever I can in my life to reach out to children in a really personal way. Although I've never been a mom, I think of myself in the capacity of sometimes needing to be an aunt. Someone willing to be present for you."

— *Julianne lives with her cats Zeke and Zoe in Seattle. She is a certified master gardener and has a passion for sustainable building and edible landscaping.*

Michael Clark remembers how one adult restored his dignity despite years of cruel teasing.

MICHAEL CLARK

The Process of Becoming

My story comes from a life-changing event on a basketball court when I was 13 and in junior high school in Howell, Michigan. I was overweight and terribly self-conscious as a young boy. I grew up in a large family, the seventh son with six older brothers. One day during an after-school basketball game, I crashed into one of my older brothers who was driving to the basket for a layup. I wasn't as coordinated as I would have liked, and my obvious bumping foul angered my brother. He yelled, "If it wasn't for you, *Porky,* I would've made that shot!"

The game ended, and as we rode away on our bikes an older boy from our neighborhood called out, "Hey, what was that name your brother called you?" I shrugged and hoped that if I didn't answer, the question would die. To my dismay he answered his own question by yelling, "Porky!" Everyone laughed, and the nickname stuck.

This nickname became so commonplace that many students in my school did not know my given first name! I tried to "make the best of it" by saying it helped me meet people and that a nickname made me approachable by helping people to feel more at ease. What a self-soothing justification. The real truth was, it hurt. The nickname became universal when I happened to take the stage at a school rally. As a homeroom representative, I was assigned to make a short address to all grades assembled. To my shock, my homeroom teacher introduced me as "Porky Clark." My humiliation was complete. As I approached the podium, the laughter and catcalls were overwhelming, yet I smiled and waved to the assembly, trying to show that I was comfortable and confident. Inside I was crying.

The following year when classes began, I was placed in an English class with a young teacher who was new to our school. With her high energy level and infectious enthusiasm, Mrs. Narda Murphy quickly became well liked. At the start of the first day of class, she began by taking the class roll call. Moving through the alphabet, she reached my name and called out, "Mike Clark?" I was shocked to hear my real first name being used in front of my peers. I eventually raised my hand and answered, "Here." No one heard my response as a whole classroom burst into laughter. My teacher look around, puzzled, and asked, "What's so funny?" A voice in the back yelled, "That's not Mike Clark, that's *Porky!*"

She slowed and simply said, "Oh, I see." Then she turned to me and said with a soft voice, "What would you like to be called?" I froze; no one had ever asked me that question before. I eventually found my voice through the snickers and answered, "Mike." "Then 'Mike' it will be," she replied with a strength that quieted the group, and she used my given first name from that point forward.

Her act alone did not bring an end to the nickname. It stuck around until my high school graduation. Yet that day in her classroom began a turnaround for me. I was drawn to this teacher, minded her rules, and worked hard for her. Beyond the class, I know she started my lifelong process of becoming "me." That morning I felt, for the first time, that something had awakened within. How could I have known that this would begin a self-rally that would transcend not only the nickname but some of life's greater obstacles to follow? My teacher's affirmation of me through endowing me with my own name sparked the more resilient part of me, allowing me to better insulate myself from hurtful comments and begin to figure out how to have an impact in life.

I eventually developed a career dedicated to youth, working for 20 years as a juvenile probation officer. Mrs. Murphy gave me the gifts of learning to be present with youth and helping to introduce them to their own "I can overcome" successful side. Her act helped me to understand that the most enduring gifts we give might well be shrouded in simple moments of respect, acknowledgment, and affirmation. I have acquired a deep personal belief that we adults have not endured hardships and reached our responsibilities solely by having our problems and shortcomings removed. Rather, we grow and attain because we each possess a unique constellation of strengths.

Mrs. Murphy was a loving presence to a young boy and helped me gain awareness of my constellation of strengths. Her simple act of naming me helped me realize I could be someone of value, someone who mattered. I will be forever grateful to this teacher I loved so much.

— *Mike Clark founded and is now director of the Center for Strength-Based Strategies in Mason, Michigan. The Center promotes the research, development, and training of strength-based strategies for adults in helping roles. Mike has traveled close to a million miles to train others on how to support young people and frequently publishes articles on his work as well.*

Close to Home

❧

Our first recollections and deepest memories are of family: the parents, the grandparents, the aunts, the uncles, the siblings and cousins with whom we share the journey of our lives. They know everything about us—both good and bad—and, if we're lucky, they love us through it all. Young people often benefit from a stand-out family member who actively encourages them to take risks, patting them on the back when they succeed, showing them how to take the next step if they fail. The stories in this section are grateful reflections from adults remembering exceptional family members who made a critical difference in their lives.

A Unique Perspective

◞

Dan Madsen wanted to try out for basketball. Not an unusual activity for a young man in junior high in 1975, but when you're only 3' tall, it presents some unique challenges. "Any other parents of a child like me might have said, 'Why don't you try something else?'" says Dan, "but not my folks."

Max and Esther Madsen knew when Dan was born in Aurora, Colorado, in 1962 that he was different. Neither a dwarf nor a midget, Dan was born with an almost unpronounceable and rare condition similar to the one that caused Abraham Lincoln to grow unusually tall, but for Dan, it worked in reverse. Dan's long bones did not grow, so his height was stunted. Throughout his childhood years, the problem required multiple surgeries in which his legs were broken and restraightened with pins. Dan spent many summers in body casts up to his waist. But Dan's current success in life as a little person (he's 4'2") started with an unusually forward-thinking doctor who told Max and Esther to take their son home and raise him normally.

"They encouraged me in all walks of life and never told me I couldn't do anything," says Dan. "They recognized the challenges

I'd face not standing as tall as everyone else, but they raised me like a normal little boy."

Dan's life was normal even if he was not. He did all the things that other children did—playing football with other kids in the neighborhood, riding his bike, fishing for crawdads. His schools were all close to home, and there were plenty of pals to play with in his neighborhood. His parents indulged his hobbies and let him plaster the walls of his room with *Star Wars* and *Star Trek* posters. His older brother, Chris, was protective but not overly. Dan's only difference from other kids was that he sometimes got teased for being short. "I remember walking home from elementary school one day, and two boys were taunting me, calling me 'Shrimp.' I got mad and swung my jacket at them and came home crying. My mom just told me to ignore them, that they weren't worth my time to get upset about. She told me I was a bigger kid than either of them for walking away and believing in myself."

Dan idolized his brother, who was a star athlete, playing on A teams in both football and basketball. Dan loved basketball. When he announced he wanted to try out for the team in middle school, Max and Esther were realistic but encouraging. "They were very supportive. They told me not to be upset if I didn't make the A team, but they never said I shouldn't do it. It would have been easy for my parents to put their arms around me to try and keep the world from hurting me. But they knew I needed to accomplish things."

So Dan tried out for the team and made the C squad. At first he was disappointed, but his parents said making any team was an accomplishment, and they encouraged him to be upbeat and positive for his teammates so they could all play their best. His parents came to all his games, congratulating him when he did well and bucking him up when he was dejected.

Later when Dan wanted to start a *Star Trek* fan club in the basement, they invested money in his venture and helped it grow into a science fiction and fantasy publishing and product business that Dan ran for nearly two decades. "My parents always supported my artistic and creative endeavors because they knew it was something I could do someday. You don't have to be 6' tall to be in the movie business or be a writer."

Dan decided to head out to Los Angeles after graduating from high school to try working as an actor. He was originally inspired by seeing an episode of the original *Star Trek* in which a little person was the star. The firm foundation he got at home gave him the courage to get himself into the offices of *Star Wars* exec George Lucas and *Star Trek* creator Gene Roddenberry, both of whom became friends and mentors. Eventually Dan would have a cameo in one of the *Star Wars* movies and meet actor Warwick Davis, another little person.

"I still remember the day I first met Gene," recalls Dan. "He sat me down in his office and we talked about being different. He told me his first thought when he created Mr. Spock was to make him a little person, but the network wouldn't let him. I was always very fond of Gene. He took a liking to me right away because I was different, and I could tell in talking with him that he truly believed everyone had a chance to be equal."

Dan, who still lives close to his parents, describes his folks as "common people who are extremely uncommon. Nobody's tooting their horn or putting them on magazine covers, but they're my heroes. They gave me the courage to do anything in life I set my sights on. They taught me to treat everyone with respect and to show compassion to those with less. They also showed me that your children come first and to always support and care for your family, no matter what."

Despite some of the difficulties Dan faced growing up, if he had it do all over again, he wouldn't go back and make himself taller. "It made me who I am and has molded the way I look at life. I'm glad I'm short, because it's given me a unique perspective on the world. You might miss something special if you're always looking at yourself. I try to pass those lessons I learned from my parents to my son."

— Dan is a freelance writer in Aurora, Colorado. He is the founder of the Official Worldwide Star Trek, Star Wars, and Lord of the Rings Fan Clubs and their official publications. He has, at various times, been a publisher, writer, actor, producer, and event promoter, but his most important job is being father and husband to Hayes and Des Madsen.

When Family Makes
All Things Possible

~

All things seem possible to a 3-year-old, so it made sense to little Eric Stillwell that he could be a chicken because he wanted to be. As he got older, of course, he realized that it wasn't possible to be a chicken, but the next best thing would be to grow up to become a farmer. In 1972, at age 10, he got his chance.

The older of two children, Eric Stillwell was already a world traveler by the time he approached 5th grade. Eric's dad, Del Stillwell, was stationed with the Air Force in Okinawa when Eric was born. Along with his younger sister, Stacey, and mom, Frankie, the family was used to pulling up roots and moving whenever Del got transferred. The public schools on military bases were populated by a cosmopolitan stew of kids from diverse backgrounds and cultures, all accustomed to moving around regularly and making new friends.

But by the time Del was slated to go to Guam for an 18-month assignment at the tail end of the Vietnam War, Eric's parents could see that it was getting harder for their children to constantly adjust as they got older. Del and Frankie decided it would be best if she and the children stayed stateside in Carlton, Oregon, where Del grew up. Living in the small rural community of 1,200 would also put the family in close proximity to the many aunts, uncles, and cousins who had lived in Carlton their whole lives.

"Starting school in a rural community with other kids who'd known each other since birth and never traveled more than a few miles from home was disconcerting," recalls Eric. "I was suddenly like a fish out of water."

Del's first cousin, Alvin Roy, and his wife, Carol, made the critical difference in Eric's life then. They went out of their way to help Eric adjust to farm life and the social complexities of a rural school. "It was a very difficult time emotionally for my mother, so I had to be strong because my dad probably told me I was the 'man of the house' while he was away," says Eric. "Alvin and Carol always tried to make sure we felt at home and that we had everything we needed."

The Roys and their extended family did all the neighborly things people do in rural communities to support Eric and his family, like bringing over fresh fruits and vegetables from the garden. Eric's family was always included with the Roys when they traveled to show animals at various county and state fairs or attended different local holiday celebrations in town, like the Fourth of July. While Frankie worked at the local meat-packing plant, Eric and Stacey would hop off the school bus in the afternoons at Carol's sister's house and stay until Frankie picked them up after work. Alvin and Carol also made sure Eric got to help out with all the animals, including chickens, ducks, rabbits, and goats, so Eric finally got his chance to learn about being a farmer firsthand. "The experience cured me of my desire to be a farmer," he says now.

The more familiar life Eric knew resumed when Del came back to the states in 1974. The family went back to life on the Air Force base, but now Eric was the only kid in his Boy Scout troop with a poultry merit badge.

"The actual experience of living on a farm in a rural community taught me a lot about responsibility, hard work, and finances," says Eric. "As I got older, I think it helped me learn things with a different point of view, not just from one outlook based on a singular life experience. I feel that I can appreciate the diversity life has to offer, especially where my wife, Debra, and I live in Los Angeles. But I'm also reminded that for all our differences, we are all very much alike and have similar feelings—sadness, worry, pleasure. We're not as different as we think."

Although Eric and Debra decided not to have children of their own when they got married, they do try to share their thirst for learning and love of travel with young people in their lives—especially family. "Whenever we travel, especially overseas, we take lots of preprinted address labels for all my young cousins, nieces, and nephews. We send back lots of postcards from all the various places we go." Eric and Debra also make sure all the kids have big, illustrated maps so they can track their travels with pins as the postcards come in to help them learn geography.

Besides being known for their travels, Eric and Debra are also known as supportive friends and generous hosts whenever anyone visits them. "I think my dad's family in Oregon really taught me about the value of extended family, but I also developed the sense that 'family' is more than blood relation. A family is made up of people you love, who are important to you, and who are part of your lives—as surely as if you share the same genetic material. So for Debra and me, our 'family' includes a wide circle of friends from all parts of the world. It makes us feel connected to a greater family of humankind. I guess when your branches and leaves are always reaching for the sun, it's nice once in a while to stop and touch your roots."

— Among Eric's many credits, he is a television writer, author, movie extra, cruise host, and event producer. He's currently an associate producer on the USA series, The Dead Zone, *and lives in Los Angeles with his wife and enthusiastic traveling companion, Debra. The two have been to several dozen countries but always try to get to the annual Memorial Day family reunion on the Roy farm, where Alvin and Carol still live and work.*

Daring to Fail

~

Edward Shanahan, Jr., rarely thought much about the fact that his mother, Monica, had a stash of fencing foils down in the basement in 1972. He was 10 and just thought it was cool to slip down there and play with them, even if he got in trouble later.

Edward, Jr., grew up in a Pittsburgh suburb called Bethel Park, the fifth of six children born to Monica and Edward Shanahan, Sr. Edward's father worked in the early days of computers, and within the mostly Italian neighborhood in which they lived, Monica seemed to be a nice, quiet stay-at-home mom. But Edward and his siblings accepted without question the fact that their mother periodically had her own television shows, including one called *Nicky's Nook* in 1958, in which some of Edward's sisters would model Halloween costumes. Or that she taught Girl Scouts the delicate art of decorating the inside of eggs, learned in apprenticeship to *the* Carl Fabergé.

"She was always trying to push the limits," recalls Edward now with some hindsight. "She was not one to be held down, for sure."

Monica, in her turn, had been influenced by her father, John Sandy, a top British fencing instructor in Peterborough, England, in the 1930s. He pushed the teenage Monica to start fencing, seeing a natural ability in his daughter. "A woman wearing pants then was practically a stoning offense in England," says Edward, "but she had the audacity to become a fencer." John's goal was to get Monica into the 1944 Olympics, but they were cancelled because of World War II.

Monica kept at it anyway and rapidly progressed from being one of the first female fencers in England to just flat out being one of the best, but most men would not fight her. "Either you beat her," Edward recalls her saying, "and everyone said, 'So what, you beat a girl,' or you got beat, in which case everyone would say derisively that you were beaten by a girl. You couldn't win either way."

Finally the Czech national champion agreed to fence Monica in an exhibition. Fencing is an incredibly fast sport, and in modern competitions, scoring is done with electronic machines to detect the touches or hits. Back in the 1940s, however, scoring relied on five sharp-eyed judges and the fencers themselves. When Monica fought the Czech champion, the first point was obviously hers—she so strongly touched her opponent's body with her foil that it bent into an arc. The judges then awarded the second point to the Czech when he clearly touched Monica with his foil. The two then fought hard for the match point. Monica felt certain she scored the winning third point by striking her opponent's shoulder, so she stepped back—the standard procedure after a hit. There was a brief pause from the judges, perhaps because they were reluctant to give match point to a woman. Her opponent also paused a moment, but then, in a gracious gesture, tapped his own shoulder where Monica's foil had hit him and said, "Touché." The crowd roared.

Monica's marriage to a British Air Force pilot soon after her fencing triumph ended in divorce, but it did bring Monica to the United States, where she met Edward's father in 1959. She gradually stopped fencing, but she never gave up following her interests and imparting to her six children extremely high standards for personal achievement.

"She raised us with a mix of praise and criticism," recalls Edward. "If we didn't do well at something, she didn't say to us, 'Boy, that stank,' but she would give us criticism that would help us be better. If you did your best and still fell short, that was okay. That meant the thing was beyond your capabilities. Then she'd help you work on your capabilities."

Edward was the only one among his siblings to take Monica up on her standing offer to teach any of them fencing (and it was a way to get his hands on those swords). None of the others could get past the first two boring weeks of no foil, just footwork. "I kept it up," says Edward, 10 years old at the time. "Even in her late 50s when she was kind of pear shaped, she was lightning fast with a foil. I'd be looking at her, my nice mom from the kitchen, and we'd square up. Suddenly she'd drop into her stance, get that ferocious look in her eyes, then whack, whack, my foil would go flying. That was fun."

Edward now tries to draw on the wisdom he gained from his mom to raise his daughter, Jessica, who at age 9 already has her own sword sized personally to her. "Jess participated in a science fair at her school where *all* the kids got a blue ribbon. I didn't think that was very helpful. That doesn't teach a child to care about excelling or even how to know when they *are* excelling. I talked with Jess about understanding that excellence is earned, not given. Winners aren't born; they make themselves winners. Losing isn't the worst thing you can do; quitting is worse, and the worst is to never have tried at all!"

⸺ Edward Shanahan's love of sword fighting led him to join the Seattle Knights two years ago. He performs with the company and occasionally portrays Sir Edward in full armor for children's birthday parties. He lives in Bremerton, Washington, with his daughter, his wife, Wendy, and his own personal collection of swords, which includes all of his mother's foils.

KEN KLIGERMAN

Thinking in Possibilities

Ken's first clear memory of Faith Virginia Babcock Kligerman was when he was just big enough to be initiated into the mysteries of hide-and-seek with his older brother, David, and some other kids from the neighborhood. Anxiously searching for a great hiding place in his paternal grandmother's home in Richmond, California, he heard Faithy whisper, "Come here." She opened up the sleeper sofa in the living room and gestured him into the open space underneath. Ken hesitated. "It's okay. There's room." Ken's first memory of his grandmother would last a lifetime. "I was scared, but I trusted her. My first impression of her was that she was a playful spirit, helping the little kid win."

Faithy was born in 1898 somewhere in the Midwest, and while she kept certain details of her life deliberately vague, she did impart intriguing tidbits to Ken during the many hours the two spent puttering around whatever house Faithy was remodeling at the time. In the early 1920s, Faithy worked the canteen at the Fox movie studio in Los Angeles where Tom Mix was a big star. In fact, Faithy said she learned to drive from Tom Mix's chauffeur. Later in life, she was an operator for Western Union, and after her retirement, she drove a big Civil Defense van for the Red Cross for many years.

By the time Ken came along, Faithy had assumed a more settled lifestyle, but not a conventional one. Ken, now a musician, performer, and songwriter, cut his teeth on performing with a little homemade box of sound effects that Faithy kept. "It had things like whoopee whistles in it, sirens, cellophane, and little metal plates that would sound like glass breaking when you'd drop them all together," Ken recalls. Faithy even had a record cutter, and she and Ken would make their own radio shows on blank 78s. Ken, who now performs as a sound effects specialist with Fantasy Theatre in Sacramento, California, still uses some of the tricks Faithy kept in that box, which remains in his possession to this day.

Faithy lived for many years in a small house in Loomis, California, on the property where Ken was living with his parents and growing up; he inherited the house from her when she died at age 98. "It was always a pleasure to wander down the road and see what she was up to," says Ken. "She built herself a little sleeping porch out back because she always preferred being outside rather than in. I follow in those footsteps. She always had something to show me out in nature, like how a certain kind of corkscrew-shaped seed would twist itself in the ground as it dried out. It was just typical for her to be amazing to me. She showed me it was good to be the eccentric person I am."

As Faithy's health declined, Ken was able to give back some of the energy and creativity his grandmother had given him even as she continued to teach him about the power of asking questions. He inspired Faithy to deal with feeling discouraged about having to move into a nursing home by telling her stories and suggesting new projects. She started crocheting booties for everyone in sight and writing poetry. When her doctor told her they'd have to amputate one of her legs because cancer necessitated removal of the bone, which would leave her limb with no usable structure, Faithy argued with him, wondering why they couldn't insert the bone of a cadaver. "She told me the doctor started to explain why that wouldn't work and then stopped, thought, and asked her to wait. He returned after making a phone call and said they would put a stainless steel rod in her leg in place of the bone. That's what they did, and it served her for many more years."

What Ken learned from Faithy is an endless fascination with self-discovery, a gift of empowerment he now imparts to children when he teaches tobacco use prevention in California public schools. "Where the Faithy-like magic comes in for me," says Ken, "is when you are guiding the kids to figure this stuff out for themselves. The plays they do are much more likely to stick in their minds because they've developed the material from their own point of view instead of having some old fuddy-duddy like me lecturing them." Ken takes kids on an eight-week odyssey through storytelling, acting, improvisation, writing, rehearsal, and performing, all based on American Lung Association curriculum for Tobacco Use Prevention Education (TUPE). He skillfully moves children from story *telling* to story *showing*, helping them reveal their own thinking about tobacco use and turning it into a full-fledged play that they write and perform themselves.

Ken says the most touching story he's heard as a result of the TUPE classes he's taught is about a student in 4th grade who was asked by her mother what she wanted for Christmas. The little girl told her mom she wanted her to stop smoking. "The mom tried and failed," says Ken, "but the little girl persisted and said she wanted the same thing for her birthday. Finally the mom succeeded. Can you imagine a 4th grader having the gut-level knowledge that smoking isn't good for her mother *and* being willing to sacrifice her Christmas and birthday presents? Wow!"

It's hard growing up being eccentric, even in a family of supportive, like-minded people, but Ken Kligerman was lucky enough to study with a master who just happened to be his own grandmother. What she taught him about following your creative instincts and being who you really are has allowed him to flourish as a performer and share those life lessons with other young people.

— Ken Kligerman facilitates performing arts workshops for all ages with special emphasis on prevention topics. He has enjoyed 33 years in all aspects of entertainment, including reupholstering theatre seats. He is a 30-year veteran and current president of the Professional Musicians of Central California, AFM Local 12.

TIM DUFFEY

The Simple Act of Sitting Down

A simple gesture by an aunt and uncle ended up having a profound impact on Tim Duffey's life at a crucial moment.

Tim had returned to his home in rural northwestern North Dakota after his first semester in college. He had been so sure when he left home that he wanted to go into pharmacy, but he quickly came to realize that this field of study wasn't really in line with his deeper interests. He wanted a closer link to what he'd learned up to that point, and social sciences seemed like it. Eventually, Tim would go into education and develop a career as a school counselor, but right now, he just didn't know how he was going to break the news to his parents that he was changing majors. They had always been so supportive, and he feared his decision would be painful for them. It didn't help that everywhere he went, folks cheerfully asked him, "How are things going at college?" He didn't know what to say.

Tim went to visit his Uncle Irv and his Aunt Lucille. Standing in their living room, Irv and Lucille also asked Tim how college was going. "When they asked the question," recalls Tim, "they did something I'll never forget—they sat down. I realized this wasn't just a passing interest or comment as it had been for so many other people—they really cared. The simple act of sitting down said to me, 'We really want to know and we will listen to whatever you say.' As we sat in comfortable easy chairs, I described how *uncomfortable* my first semester had been. The coursework wasn't engaging, and I was struggling to see how I would ever be happy as a pharmacist. They listened without judgment, helped me clarify my thoughts and concerns, and provided me a safe place to ponder possibilities. It was a true gift."

Feeling comfortable enough to tell Irv the truth was born of a lifetime of Tim's being in the presence of a trusted adult. Growing up the youngest of six children surrounded by extended family, Tim's early years were spent on a farm. Later the family lived near the Fort Union Trading Post, a unit of Theodore Roosevelt National Park where his dad was a caretaker of the historic site. Tim spent lots of time with family, siblings, and friends hunting for artifacts and historic relics.

"I never felt unsafe in any way," says Tim. "It was a wonderful place to grow up with lots of opportunity to explore my environment the way young people love to do. My family provided me with a feeling of security and sense of wonder about everything around me, so it was pretty natural that I'd spend time finding new and interesting places. I loved realizing that the history of the region was real—I could touch it. I learned to love history and gained an appreciation for the importance of understanding what led up to a set of events."

Uncle Irv was one of the most influential people in Tim's early life. "He was very soft spoken," says Tim, "quiet, always a very reassuring, calming influence. He was involved in a lot of youth-oriented activities as a Boy Scout leader, active with youth members of Civil Air Patrol, and engaged with young people in his congregation. He and Lucille were very caring and principled people. It just emanated from them."

Tim's most vivid memory of spending time with Irv was the one summer day they took a canoeing trip on the Missouri River after Tim was in grade 7. "At the time I had never set foot in a canoe before, and it was a pretty big deal to go. I remember thinking how cool it was that I was asked to do this alone with someone I really admired. It didn't seem that adults often sought chances to take me individually on extended adventures like this. I really looked forward to what I knew would be a beautiful, long day on the river with no distractions, learning new skills, and seeing things I'd never seen in quite this way before."

Where the two would put in the canoe, the Missouri River runs fast. The water is often turbulent with dangerous whirl-pools that have long challenged light watercraft. It was a warm summer day, and as Tim found himself actually standing on the shoreline, the murky water suddenly seemed ominous and their boat very small in comparison to the river. Uncle Irv started with some basic instruction in canoe strokes and critical lessons on such things as getting in and out of the craft without ending up in the water.

"I started out in the front of the canoe," laughs Tim. "I know now it's because that's the least risky spot to put someone new to the art of canoeing. By the end of the day, when the river slowed down as we approached the backwater of Lake Sakakawea, I was in the back of the canoe using my newfound skills in paddling to direct our progress—and without mishap, I might add! I had started the day as a novice, but I ended it with a real sense of accomplishment."

What the young man remembered most about that day, however, was that his Uncle Irv was interested in what he had to say. "There wasn't anything really tough or awful going on in my life. My growing up was actually pretty idyllic. I was actively engaged in school, had a sense of belonging in my community, and had strong family support, but I had a sense that he was providing an opportunity to connect. Even though my life experiences weren't filled with trauma or extreme misfortune, I was still 13 and dealing with all the questions of belonging and wonderment about where my life would lead that every 13-year-old goes through."

Tim would grow up enjoying canoe paddling in his adult life and would impart the skills he learned on the Missouri that day to his three children. But the legacy of his lifelong relationship with his uncle and the profound memory of this particular river trip was the experience of having the undivided attention of a caring, principled role model. "The day's conversation just seemed general and open, driven by whatever it was I had to say. Throughout the day, Uncle Irv asked about my school life, what I was interested in and cared about, and what was most important to me. He was a 'listening ear' of the first order. I just still have such a strong memory of being in the presence of someone who really cared about what I had to say."

Reflecting on the canoeing trip with his Uncle Irv, Tim says, "I look back on that day on the river and I have a real sense that it wasn't accidental, that Irv set up the opportunity to have all that time and space for conversation. He never heard of Developmental Assets or even positive youth development, but he *lived* it. Somehow he had the wisdom and insight to live his life with a commitment to being that kind of positive presence to all kinds of kids."

As Tim went on to work with young people as a guidance counselor, raise his own three children, and now train youth, he came to see his part in passing on what Irv gave him. "Now it's my task—in his honor—to pass the baton to other young people by being that kind of presence for them. Far too many of our young people don't see that many adults *are* really interested in who they are, in what they believe, in what's important to them. But I remember a sunny summer day on the Missouri River that reminds me every day how powerful a listening ear can be."

— Tim Duffey is the training manager for Vision Training Associates in Maine, which coordinates all speaking, training, and presentation events for Search Institute. Tim lives with Donna, his wife of 28 years, in southern Maine. He has transferred his canoe experience to sea kayaking and continues to enjoy outdoor experiences like hiking and camping while using some of the camping gear that belonged to late Uncle Irv.

*Mervlyn Kitashima remembers how
her grandmother gave her self-worth
when others were critical.*

MERVLYN KITASHIMA

Almost Done

～

Growing up on the Hawaiian island of Kauai, I was culturally wrong. My mother was Hawaiian, born and raised on the island, and my father was from New Jersey. My mother had three children from a first marriage, my father had six children, and then my parents proceeded to have four more. Cultures didn't mix back when I was born in 1955. We looked different. We weren't Caucasian, or White, or *haole* (the Hawaiian word for foreigner), and we weren't Hawaiian. We were different, so we were culturally wrong. And we were treated differently.

But one of the things that made a difference for me was that I was fortunate to have caring and supportive people throughout all of my life. A lot of times it wasn't my parents because they were too busy needing to take care of their own stuff. For me, the first and foremost was my grandma. A lot of us have wonderful grandmas and grandpas and aunties and uncles. Mine was my Grandma Kahaunaele, who is my mother's mother. Grandma Kahaunaele lived down the road from us, and when things got really bad at home, we would end up at Grandma and Grandpa Kahaunaele's home. We spent many, many nights at Grandma and Grandpa Kahaunaele's. That's where we stayed when my mom was in the institution, because my father couldn't handle all of us.

I remember understanding back then that we were "those children." You know who "those children" are—the ones parents talk about saying, "I don't want you playing with 'those children,'" or "I don't want you going to 'those people's' house." We were "those children" that nobody wanted around. I don't know if it's because we were different, or because we were always dirty; I don't know why, but we were. That's how I felt. But my Grandma was a wonderful, quiet Hawaiian woman. She didn't say much, so I don't remember her voice, but she had this incredible heart. My Grandma Kahaunaele never treated me like one of "those children."

Hawaii is red dirt. It's red dirt, and it stains. It's terrible. My Grandma was immaculately clean. Her house was spotless and shiny. She washed and ironed pillowcases, underwear, T-shirts. That's how she was. You can imagine what she thought when she saw us after we'd cut through the park or the cane field. And if there was water in the irrigation ditches, we'd jump in there and catch toads and tadpoles and whatever else there was. Then we ended up at her house. She must have said, "Oh, my golly. Here they come." But if she thought it, she never said it. Not once do I remember her saying to me, "You are filthy. Go home. I don't want you here." Instead, she would dump us in the outside tub to wash off the red dirt and then let us in the house.

My Grandma Kahaunaele was the only person who would comb my hair. Hawaiian girls always have long hair, and I had long hair, but it was always tangled and dirty. I remember sitting in the playground in 1st grade and wondering why my head was so itchy. It's because it was so dirty. Back then I'd scratch and scratch. Grandma Kahaunaele was the one who would wash my hair, and she was the only one who would take the tangles out. She would sit me down on her knee, and she'd have this giant, yellow comb. She'd patiently take every tangle out of my hair. And for anyone who's had long, tangled hair, with a comb going through it—not fun, you know? Your head is yanking as it gets caught, and I'd be crying. She would say, "Almost *pau,* almost *pau.*" *Pau* means finished. "Almost done." She would eventually finish, and I remember feeling clean and pretty, and I remember feeling like maybe somebody cares for me, even for just a little while.

My Grandma Kahaunaele had a wooden leg. A car ran over her toes when she was a child and the infection grew and grew until they took her leg off just below the knee. She'd have to put on about six pairs of socks for padding, and then she'd buckle her leg on. I can still see her doing it at the edge of her bed. At night when she would go to bed, she would take off the leg and stand it at the post of her bed.

I remember waking up at night at her house, having nightmares and crying and feeling afraid, looking for someone to care for me. The image I will never forget is this woman crawling on her hands and knees down the hall to come and make sure I was okay—because she had no leg.

Each of us needs to build into our own life and the lives of others this kind of caring and support. We each need someone who will love us without condition, regardless of what we look like, how dirty we are, what kind of clothes we wear, the color of our skin, hair, or eyes. Unconditional love—every single one of us needs this.

— *Mervlyn Kitashima was one of 700 babies born on the island of Kauai studied by Emmy Werner and Ruth Smith for more than*

40 years, tracking the impact of what made a difference in the lives of children. She is currently the district coordinator for the Parent-Community Networking Center with the Hawaii Department of Education. This story is excerpted from a speech Kitashima gave in 1997 at the University of Maryland and is adapted and reprinted with permission from Mentoring for Resiliency: Setting Up Programs to Move Youth from Stressed to Success, *published by Resiliency In Action, San Diego, CA, 2000, p.60.*

Giving Back

~

Life's lessons are not always easy, but the right guide can often help a child or young person navigate events with grace and understanding. Young people don't necessarily have to face serious adversity to benefit from the shared gifts of an adult's experience. But if they do, the solid presence of at least one trusted adult can make a powerful statement that will resonate for years to come. The stories in this section chronicle the deliberate intervention by some key adults during difficult times and relate how each storyteller turned a situation into a quiet opportunity to give back some of what they had received.

SHARON BRIDWELL

The Ornament Lady

It happens routinely at Sharon Bridwell's house: There's a knock at the door, and standing outside are a couple of neighborhood children. "Can we come in and color? You have the best ideas and supplies." Or she steps out to the mailbox and several children call out, "When can we do another project?" Or the doorbell rings and a shy 11-year-old neighbor says, "I just came by to say hello." A day in the life of the Ornament Lady.

The story of how this nickname came about amuses Sharon. Several years ago, she and her husband were new to a young community in Las Vegas, Nevada, where few residents really knew each other yet. Since they were often home during the day, Sharon and her husband noticed the kids in the neighborhood just milling about. They struck upon the idea of introducing themselves and inviting young people to bring a friend and come make a Christmas ornament if it was okay with their parents.

Children found that designing ornaments was fun, and Sharon got to know them while they all worked together. Word got around the neighborhood, and the doorbell kept ringing. "About two dozen cheap blank ornaments and a bunch of glue pens later," says Sharon, "we knew many of the kids in the neighborhood. That New Year's we gave a party, and many of the parents came to meet these people their kids said were 'so cool.'"

So she became known as the Ornament Lady. But that was only the beginning of her relationships and activities with her young neighbors. For example, shortly after the events of September 11, 2001, Sharon's 9-year-old neighbor, Tyler, came over and asked her to teach him to play "God Bless America" on the piano. Sharon only plays by ear but was happy to help. Tyler quickly picked the song up and has been coming to Sharon's house every Saturday morning since then for more of these "lessons." Observes Sharon, "Some Saturdays we talk about things that are on Tyler's mind more than we play piano."

Where does Sharon Bridwell get the energy for this? From four adults way back in high school in suburban Atlanta who helped Sharon survive a challenging family life.

At the time, Sharon was an accomplished student, both academically and in extracurricular activities, even voted "Most Likely to Succeed." But her parents' bitter divorce when she was 16 was only one of a host of problems at home. "My mom was recovering from colon cancer and became an alcoholic," recalls Sharon. "My younger brother and I never knew what was coming on any given day. For me, taking care of my brother became a serious responsibility."

Starting with high school guidance counselor Marguerite Bond, a core group of adults at the school took Sharon under their collective wings, checking in with her every day. "They celebrated my achievements, bragged endlessly about me, extended invitations for dinner, and spearheaded opportunities targeted just for me." History teacher George Carden, for example, sponsored Sharon's application to the summer Georgia Governor's Honors program in Social Studies when she was a sophomore. Having the opportunity to attend this month-long camp stretched Sharon socially, but, she says, "I loved it and thrived there. I became more confident that I had skills and could do whatever I wanted."

Ellen Risner, Sharon's cheerleading advisor, touched bases with her every day after school whether there was a practice or not. When Sharon faced an intimidating talent performance in the Miss CHS contest, Ellen slipped her a note that read "Look up and smile! Enjoy it—you're beautiful!" "I still have that note," says Sharon.

And when Sharon was given the first government grant (secured by Marguerite) for a student to attend an international exchange, her sociology teacher, Jan Christopher, lent Sharon clothes to wear on her ten-day trip to Brazil, representing her school and the state of Georgia. Sharon's mom wasn't able to help her explore college plans, so Marguerite made sure Sharon pursued good options and went to college on scholarship with outstanding letters of recommendation from these extraordinary adults and others.

More than 25 years later, Sharon has stayed connected with several of these supportive adults, in some cases still seeking their advice and taking the time to thank them. "I realize now that I was not the only youth they took time to help, but my life certainly would have been different without them. I worked for many years in an aggressive marketing career and didn't have much time to acknowledge important people, but now I have the time. Both to say thank you and to give back."

While Sharon has two stepdaughters, she hasn't had children of her own. "That's why it's so easy for me to pinch hit and celebrate the kids around me," she says. "It feels good." In addition to nurturing youth in the neighborhood, Sharon and her husband, Gene, have done significant volunteer work with nonprofit groups dedicated to improving the lives of community youth. Whether they come into contact with youth in the community or just around the neighborhood, Sharon and Gene always find that young people respond positively to any notice and appreciate discussions about their opinions, experiences, talents, and goals.

"Here's what I've learned," says Sharon. "Although working on a project to create something provides a reason to be together, it's more about the interaction with a young person during the project. Every time you talk to the same kid, no matter how long, you create more of a relationship for the time, down the road, when the conversation will be about something of greater perspective or importance. When I see that young person again, I try to recall and ask about something that seemed important to them the last time. This goes deep with me, because I build many beautiful connections with both young and old, and I'm a better person for it."

In addition to developing positive relationships with young people in her neighborhood, Sharon Bridwell enjoys her 8- and 12-year-old nieces and 6-year-old nephew. She and Gene have lived many places in the U.S. and traveled throughout the world, moving to Las Vegas after living and working in Switzerland for many years. Sharon now has her own business at home making and selling purses and likes working with the community's local asset-building initiative, Raising Nevada.

DEBBIE DEVINE

The "Wow" Moment

As each of her children had transitioned through the elementary grades of their California schools, Debbie Devine had always shown up at the principal's office at the start of the year, asking to be put to work as a volunteer.

But as her son was ready to start middle school in fall 2001, she didn't know whether they'd need her at the new school; she had heard people murmur that kids this age don't want their parents involved anymore. She was relieved to hear from her son's new 6th-grade teacher that that wasn't true. Although her son's teacher didn't need her in the classroom, another teacher did. So that year, Debbie partnered with a woman named Diana Powell and the two women worked together to start an early morning math club for students who were struggling with math. But it took some time to get it rolling.

"Their self-esteem was at rock bottom," says Debbie. "They'd have their sweatshirt hoods pulled up over their faces, saying things like, 'I'm so stupid, I can't do anything.' So we just tried to get to know them at first. Eventually, the hoods came down, and they started to stand a little taller. And then we started working on math. Their teachers noticed they were participating more in class, and as their self-esteem improved, so did their grades."

Debbie felt that she was making a difference, but it wasn't until she attended a series of workshops on asset building through Project Cornerstone in San Jose that she learned of the Developmental Assets, which explained *why* she was having an impact. And the more she understood the positive qualities and opportunities that young people need to succeed in life, the more she understood just how she had been helped when she was young.

"You go back through your own childhood and realize you've had some similar experiences to these kids you're working with. I'm pretty well adjusted, but I found some of what we were learning painful. I realized that there were certain adults who had plucked me out of some of the messes I was into as a kid, just as some of the kids in the research could point to that one adult or incident that put them on the right track. That was my 'wow' moment. One person *can* make a difference."

The depth of Debbie's experiences working with students began to undergo a profound change, and she found herself reaching out to more young people in a more intentional way.

One Wednesday morning, she arrived to get the Zero Period Math Club started. Classes start later, at 9 AM, on Wednesday mornings, so the math club starts at 7:15 AM. One of the students in the club accidentally cut his finger fairly deeply and Debbie couldn't find a first-aid kit, so she took the student out front to her van to get a bandage. "As we were returning, I noticed a boy who was pacing back and forth on the sidewalk outside the gates. He seemed kind of agitated, and at first it appeared his face was sweating profusely. When I got closer I realized it was tears, and he was trying to wipe them off. It was only 36 degrees when I left my house that morning. This child had no jacket or sweatshirt. He was only wearing a dress-type shirt, and it was a bit too small."

Debbie recognized the boy as a new student in another teacher's class from the day before. When she spoke to him, he blurted out, "I didn't know, I didn't know!" Apparently no one had told him of the late-start Wednesdays. "I had my student—the one with the cut finger—take him to the bathroom and let him wash up. My student brought him back to Math Club, and he joined us for the morning. His hands were so cold he couldn't even hold the pencil. It kept slipping from his grasp. I just sat there holding his hands until they warmed up."

Debbie and the other students explained the bell schedules for the day. Later she slipped home and "stole" one of her son's sweatshirts to bring to the boy at school. A month later, he was still often wearing the sweatshirt, and Debbie noticed that he had become fast friends with the student who cut his finger.

On another occasion, Debbie faced a personal barrier when she was asked to help an 8th-grade student for the first time. One of the teachers had a student who needed help with his Rite of Passage Experience or ROPES project. All 5th and 8th graders are required to choose and research a topic for this project, then do a 10-minute presentation to a committee. "I had felt intimidated by these 8th-grade human beings," says Debbie. "They seemed bigger and scarier to me, so I was very nervous. I wanted everything to go right."

She was asked to help a student who had not yet turned in any of the required work for the project. "He had trouble looking me in the eye at first, but I started trying to gauge where he needed help and then provide some of the structure. Eventually he started to relax and look me in the eye. I realized that he actually already had the whole project about the invention of photography in his head. He became more energized and focused. He just needed some one-on-one help to get that."

By overcoming her remaining fears and stereotypes about young people and taking new steps to really reach out at a deeper level, Debbie realized that relationships with youth go both ways. "Originally I stumbled through the math club, but now I have a focus. I see it's my job and my mission to fix something when I see it's not right. I've learned that youth are people, and they've learned that not all adults are creeps. They'll believe that someone will be around if they need help."

➤ Debbie Devine lives with her 13-year-old son, Christopher, 9-year-old daughter, Kimberly, and her "poor husband," David, who puts up with Debbie's other passion—animals—by sharing the household with two rabbits, a snake, and a dog. Also a former Girl Scout, Debbie is a Girl Scout leader who shares with her daughter the outdoor skills she learned from her own mom.

HENK NEWENHOUSE

A Quiet, Consistent Presence

You couldn't miss Henk Newenhouse that first crisp, fall Saturday in 1999 that he came to watch the local high school varsity soccer game. Henk's hard to miss wherever he goes in his tiny adopted hometown of Gotham, Wisconsin. There's his completely white hair and the remnants of the Dutch accent left from his childhood in Holland. And there are times the 78-year-old survivor of the Nazi occupation of his village during WWII makes a point to stand out: for example, when he solo pickets for peace outside the post office. But this Saturday, he stood out in a way he had not anticipated—he was the only soccer fan out to watch the game who was not related to any of the 18 players on the field.

Henk's appearance at the soccer field was just one of the many ways he had been demonstrating his support for the young people of this rural area since settling on a farm there with his wife, Linda, in 1984. After his own three children were grown, Henk would time his morning walk to coincide with neighborhood children waiting for the school bus so he could get to know them. Henk also mediated more than 1,200 divorces involving children.

However, too freely giving out his phone number to teens in need of advice finally overwhelmed him, so he searched for other options. He and Linda adopted the Gotham Go Getters 4-H club for several years, hosting meetings and teaching gardening. But something about attending those soccer games struck a chord in Henk. He'd grown up with the sport in Europe and its "stepchild" status to football at the high school appealed to the maverick in him. But there was a deeper impetus for his interest in young people, something further back that the elderly man was trying to reclaim.

The year Henk Newenhouse should have started high school, the Nazis occupied the small village of Kapelle on the island Zuid-Beveland in the utmost southern part of Holland, where he lived with his parents and older brother. At a time when most young men are entering high school with a sense of optimism and adventure, Henk was forced to avoid school so he would not be taken hostage. The school was commandeered to house troops, and teachers were sometimes killed or had to flee. At his parents' insistence, Henk's brother escaped to Amsterdam to avoid being drafted by the Germans. Constant fear kept many people locked in their homes. Henk and his mother, Johanna Nieuwenhuize-de Kraay, spent long hours alone together, often in the dark when the power went out. To pass the time, the young boy and his mother began a series of conversations that would change both their lives. "It was my mother's awakening to politics and her sharing that with me that *totally* changed my life," Henk recalls.

The oldest daughter of extremely progressive parents who believed in education, Johanna was a teacher by trade, so she naturally turned to education to survive the war. To express her outrage at the German occupation of Holland, she joined a local homemaker's association that quietly began to educate themselves about politics.

"They were just a group of country women who didn't think of themselves as particularly brave," says Henk. "They read and talked and then discussed things with their children. There was no big morality that hit you over the head. They just talked about what the Germans were doing, and not just how they were treating the Jews, but also how they treated the mentally ill and gays. My mother really created in me an awareness of the moral issues of politics. Since I couldn't go to school, I had a lot of time to think. Some people would say that as a result, I became a troublemaker, but from my point of view, I became a seeker of the truth."

Emerging from those dark years, Henk eventually finished his education and set out—often alone—for the truth. He became an advocate for the mentally ill, spent time in prison for refusing to join the Dutch army, worked at the United Nations, and, after immigrating to the U.S., got fired for standing up to corporate fraud. Starting his own educational film company gave Henk the freedom to settle in Gotham and renew the rural farm life he'd lost during the war, but there was still something missing. That high school experience. "I guess I was seeking that out in my old age," says Henk. "I enjoy very much being around enthusiastic young people."

After five years of steadfastly attending soccer games since that first Saturday, Henk has been given back more than he ever anticipated, and being the only nonfamily member in the crowd has earned him a special status. "Each year, I get to know all 18 families on the bench and, through them, most members of the team. Now, whenever I go shopping, a current or past soccer player invariably changes my oil, checks my groceries, or waves at me while mowing the right-of-way. I've been invited to graduation parties and notified of hospitalizations or successful college entrances. I know a lot of teenagers and they know me. It feels absolutely wonderful to go into town and do my errands and have four or five teens say, 'Hi, Henk!'"

"Henk is a very kind person who goes out of his way to help anyone who needs it," says Mark Harper, a former 4-H'er who now teaches middle school and rents a house from Henk a few doors down from him on Slow Lane. Mark describes the experience of working for Henk during the summer along with his brothers as not just a job, but more of a lifetime's involvement as friends. Mark says Henk didn't just invite him over to learn gardening, but also took time to visit Mark's grandparents as they aged. "Henk works just as hard as my brothers and me," says Mark. "He has shown us that hard work and persistence pay off, no matter what you're doing."

Henk's premier fan status now earns him an invitation to the annual soccer banquet. At the most recent banquet he attended, Henk was stunned to hear the words of Nick Hallett, the player who received the evening's highest award and who was asked to say a few words at the end of the event. Nick rose shyly, paused a moment, then stood up straight and said, "I want to thank Henk for coming to all our games. It meant a lot to me."

"Driving home," says Henk, "I realized how much *his* statement meant to *me*. I was truly moved."

⏤ *Henk Newenhouse, Ph.D., was born and educated in Holland, moving to the United States in 1955 to work at the United Nations. After working as advertising manager for Charles Pfizer & Co.*

and account executive for Procter and Gamble's Crest Toothpaste, he became owner of Perennial Education, Inc. He now divides his time among multiple activities, including volunteering for the Circuit Court, writing a column for an English magazine, officiating at 50 weddings a year, and going to soccer games.

Here I share my own story about
trying to make a difference.

DEBORAH FISHER

Camp Victory

~

My heart pounded in my chest as I stood with several dozen other women waiting for the school buses to arrive that Friday evening at Camp Victory. Our weeks of training and preparation were over, and our trial-by-fire was about to begin. Word spread that the buses were turning down the dusty road toward camp, full of young girls from age 10 to 17, all from a cluster of small communities on the western Washington coast. From Friday night until Sunday afternoon, these girls would do the things most kids do when they go to summer camp—play, have camp-fires, sing songs, walk the beach, and stay up too late. What made this weekend camp different, however, was the fact that each of these girls—and many of the counselors—had been sexually abused. Camp Victory would be a respite and perhaps, for some of the girls, the first step toward healing from that abuse.

Camp Victory is run by a very committed group of professional and community women—many also survivors—who recognize the need of these young girls in their community. Year-long fundraising activities support the camp and pay for scholarships for girls to attend. Camp counselors are carefully recruited through professional and personal associations, and we all underwent rigorous training to prepare us for the emotional experience of being in camp.

Being a counselor at Camp Victory isn't for everyone. Much of our training was geared toward understanding our past experience and being able to hold it in check so our own feelings wouldn't intrude on any of the girls. Our job was to maintain boundaries of personal and emotional safety for the girls at all times.

The focus of our work, besides just having fun with the campers, was the assignment to each of us of a "buddy." Each woman was paired with a child who was to be our special charge during camp. The girls all knew they would have an adult "buddy," but they also knew that our role was to be only as present as they wanted us to be. We were not told any of the details of our buddy's situation. The girls could tell us as much or as little as they wished to share. We were to take all our cues from them as to how much involvement they wanted from us.

I still remember the dark, piercing eyes of the 11-year-old girl who was my buddy. We spent the entire weekend in each other's vicinity, but she kept a wary distance between us. She allowed me to attend to the specific functions of her care—helping her get up in the morning, making sure she got a bandage when she skinned her shins—but most of the time, she seemed to revel in being able to skip ahead and reject most of my attentions. I could see her out of the corner of my eye, watching to see how I'd react. It was probably one of the few times in her life she had felt that sense of control, which is exactly what the weekend was designed to do. So, distantly tethered, we made our way through the weekend.

It was an intense, meaningful three days. The camp's organizers had designed a series of activities that, on one level, gave the girls fun things to do, but on another, allowed them to ac-knowledge and release their feelings. One afternoon in the bright sunshine, I stood near my buddy in a big circle with everyone else. One of the women led us through some self-defense moves, culminating in all the girls learning to shout no in loud voices they probably didn't know they had. We made tie-dyed T-shirts, which for some of the girls would be the only new clothes they'd get that year. Some of the girls made spirit dolls out of fabric and beads, using art to make effigies representing their experiences. On Saturday night, armed with flashlights, we went on a moon-light walk on the beach, everyone linked by hands and hearts. At the bonfire later that night, some girls burned their effigies and simply wept in their buddy's arms or asked to be held.

My buddy maintained her distance. She always stayed within my sight, which was one of the camp's ground rules for buddies, but she often kept her back to me, concentrating on animated conversations with the new friends she had made. My arms ached to hold her, give her comfort. I wanted to tell her to hold on, reassure her that she would have a brighter future.

Our hearts were aching on Sunday afternoon when we had to let all these precious beings go. We each felt a sense of sweet, unspoken connection with our buddies. All of us hoped that by our simple presence, we had imparted the message to these girls during the weekend that they could survive, they *would* survive, and someday they would heal.

The bright yellow school buses returned, and the time finally came to say good-bye. Suddenly I felt two small arms wrap themselves around me like steel bands. I felt the moisture of tears sinking into my sweatshirt. I hugged my buddy back just as fiercely, then she was gone. Recalling that moment even now still brings tears to my eyes.

I'll probably never know whether the actions I took with that little girl so many summers ago had a lasting impact for her of any kind, let alone the one I intended. But it might have. It's easy to go through our days thinking our gestures with children don't really make a difference, but the stories in this book tell us otherwise.

— *Deborah Fisher is the author of this book and a freelance journalist specializing in writing about children and families. A former legal affairs reporter for Minnesota Public Radio and a contributor to National Public Radio, she has also implemented asset-building projects in the Puget Sound region of Washington. This is her third book for Search Institute.*

From the Author: "Tell Me *Your* Story"

Does reading these stories inspire you to think about who was there for you at a critical time? Have you been able to turn around and give to young people in your life the gifts that you received from positive adults? I'd like to hear about your story for a new collection. You can write up a draft of your story to send to me or just share some highlights and we can talk about it together. Here are the high points of what I'd like to know:

- The context in which the story happened—where you lived, how old you were, how things were for you leading up to the events of the story.
- Who is the critical person who acted in your story? What was he or she like?
- What was the turning point in your story?
- What did this experience do for you? What did the experience mean? How did things change?
- What did you learn from this experience?
- How have you given back to others from what you learned?

Include contact information so I can reach you to discuss your story. Please reach me through my Web site, www.deborahfisher. org. I'll look forward to hearing from you!

Top 10 Tips for Connecting with Young People

1. *Say hello and smile.* Many young people are used to being ignored by adults—surprise them by standing out from the crowd!

2. *Ask them their names.* Watch a young person's face light up when you show enough interest to want to know who he or she is.

3. *Be yourself.* Young people will respond to you better if they sense you are being genuine.

4. *Ask them about things that are of interest to them.* Nothing will help trigger conversation more than your questions about something a young person is interested in.

5. *Simply listening will give you ideas of what to talk about.* Once the subject is apparent, make positive comments about their interests or abilities.

6. *Follow up your initial questions with questions or observations that show you're listening.* If a young person talks about being into skateboarding, ask where his or her favorite skate park is.

7. *Never assume that the mind you're talking to is closed.* Just because young people dress or act differently from you doesn't mean they're not taking in what you've said.

8. *Don't expect young people to reach out to you.* Take the initiative as an adult to reach out to them.

9. *Draw from your own memories.* Think back to someone who made a difference in your life and how she or he connected with you.

10. *Keep at it!* Not every attempt to connect with young people will have immediate results, but remain earnest and speak from your heart.

What Are the Developmental Assets?

The Developmental Assets are spread across eight broad areas of human development. These categories paint a picture of the positive things—the developmental "nutrients"—that all young people need to grow up healthy and responsible. The first four asset categories focus on external structures, relationships, and activities that create a positive environment for young people:

 Support—Young people need to be surrounded by people who love, care for, appreciate, and accept them. They need to know that they belong and that they are not alone.

 Empowerment—Young people need to feel valued and valuable. This happens when youth feel safe, when they believe that they are liked and respected, and when they contribute to their families and communities.

 Boundaries and Expectations—Young people need the positive influence of peers and adults who encourage them to be and do their best. Youth also need clear rules about appropriate behavior and consistent, reasonable consequences for breaking those rules.

 Constructive Use of Time—Young people need opportunities—outside of school—to learn and develop new skills and interests, and to spend enjoyable time interacting with other youth and adults.

The next four categories reflect internal values, skills, and beliefs that young people also need to develop to fully engage with and function in the world around them:

Commitment to Learning—Young people need a variety of learning experiences, including the desire for academic success, a sense of the lasting importance of learning, and a belief in their own abilities.

 Positive Values—Young people need to develop strong guiding values or principles, including caring about others, having high standards for personal character, and believing in protecting their own well-being.

 Social Competencies—Young people need to develop the skills to interact effectively with others, to make difficult decisions and choices, and to cope with new situations.

 Positive Identity—Young people need to believe in their own self-worth, to feel that they have control over the things that happen to them, and to have a sense of purpose in life as well as a positive view of the future.

The Challenge

The good news is that the assets are powerful and that everyone can build them (intentionally trying to help youth develop these strengths is *building assets*). Search Institute's research shows that the more assets young people have, the more likely they are to make positive choices in life and the less likely they are to use tobacco, alcohol, or other drugs. The challenge for all of us is that most young people aren't experiencing enough of them.

For more information on the Developmental Assets and how you can build them for and with young people, visit www.search-institute.org or call 800-888-7828 for a free information packet.

About Search Institute

Search Institute is an independent, nonprofit, nonsectarian organization whose mission is to provide leadership, knowledge, and resources to promote healthy children, youth, and communities. The institute collaborates with others to promote long-term organizational and cultural change that supports its mission.